CAMBRIDGE SKILLS FOR FLUENCY
Series Editor: Adrian Doff

COMHAIRLE CHONTAE ÁTHA CLIATH TH

Reading 2

Simon Greenall
Diana Pye

CAMBRIDGE
UNIVERSITY PRESS

PUBLISHED BY THE PRESS SYNDICATE OF THE UNIVERSITY OF CAMBRIDGE
The Pitt Building, Trumpington Street, Cambridge, United Kingdom

CAMBRIDGE UNIVERSITY PRESS
The Edinburgh Building, Cambridge CB2 2RU, UK   http://www.cup.cam.ac.uk
40 West 20th Street, New York, NY 10011–4211, USA   http://www.cup.org
10 Stamford Road, Oakleigh, Melbourne 3166, Australia

© Cambridge University Press 1991

This book is in copyright. Subject to statutory exception
and to the provisions of relevant collective licensing agreements,
no reproduction of any part may take place without
the written permission of Cambridge University Press.

First published 1991
Sixth printing 1999

Printed in the United Kingdom at the University Press, Cambridge

ISBN 0 521 34675 4

BH

Contents

Map of the book

Unit	Function/Structural areas	Vocabulary areas	Reading strategies
1 Have you got a spirit of adventure?	Describing personal characteristics.	Sports and leisure activities; personal characteristics.	Predicting; dealing with unfamiliar words; extracting main ideas.
2 Weather facts	Present simple; past simple; making predictions.	Weather.	Predicting; extracting main ideas; dealing with unfamiliar words.
3 A home in a foreign land	Talking about the past; past simple.	Personal history.	Predicting; extracting main ideas; dealing with unfamiliar words.
4 A room of my own	Describing objects and furniture.	Houses, rooms and furniture.	Predicting; extracting main ideas; understanding text organisation; dealing with unfamiliar words; evaluating the text.
5 Childhood dreams	Talking about the past; past simple; past continuous.	Personal history of famous people.	Predicting; extracting main ideas; dealing with unfamiliar words.
6 Mr Jones	Describing people's appearance and characteristics.	Physical appearance and personal characteristics.	Predicting; extracting main ideas; inferring; dealing with unfamiliar words; understanding text organisation.
7 Avoiding close encounters	Giving advice; past simple.	Wildlife.	Predicting; extracting main ideas; dealing with unfamiliar words; understanding text organisation; reading for specific information.
8 School	Describing feelings and impressions.	Childhood memories.	Extracting main ideas; reacting to the text; reading for specific information.
9 2010	Talking about the future; describing objects and technological devices; future simple.	Technology of the future.	Predicting; extracting main ideas; dealing with unfamiliar words.

Unit	Function/Structural areas	Vocabulary areas	Reading strategies
10 A slip of the pen		News items, advertisements.	Reacting to the text; evaluating the text.
11 Drawing on the right side of the brain	Describing intellectual qualities and creative skills.	Right and left brain.	Predicting; dealing with unfamiliar words; reacting to the text.
12 My time of life	Describing change; talking about state and routine; present simple; present perfect.	Growing old.	Evaluating the text; reading for specific information; dealing with unfamiliar words.
13 The tramp and the farmer	Telling a story; past simple; past continuous.		Predicting; inferring; linking ideas.
14 Fear	Describing feelings and emotional reactions.	Fears, feelings.	Extracting main ideas; dealing with unfamiliar words; linking ideas; reacting to the text.
15 In search of the little people	Describing appearance; talking about the past.	Fairies, legends.	Predicting; extracting main ideas; dealing with unfamiliar words; reading for specific information.
16 Man's inhumanity to women		Women and the English language.	Reading for specific information; inferring; dealing with unfamiliar words; linking ideas.
17 Cats	Describing animal characteristics; present simple; past simple.	Animal behaviour.	Extracting main ideas; reading for specific information; evaluating the text; reacting to the text.
18 City scenes	Talking about cities; describing characteristics.	Towns, feelings.	Predicting; reading for specific information; reacting to the text; evaluating the text.
19 Eccentrics	Talking about routine activities and behaviour; present simple.	Unusual interests and behaviour.	Predicting; dealing with unfamiliar words; reacting to the text; extracting main ideas.
20 The Misanthrope	Talking about past events; past simple, present perfect; talking about obligation and prohibition.	Rules and regulations.	Predicting; extracting main ideas; evaluating the text; reacting to the text.

Thanks

We would like to thank:

Jeanne McCarten, Alison Silver, Lindsay White, Peter Ducker and everybody at Cambridge University Press for making the book possible.

Adrian Doff and other readers for their extremely helpful comments on the first draft.

Pat Pringle for supplying some of the passages.

The authors and publishers would like to thank all the institutions who helped pilot the material.

1 | Have you got a spirit of adventure?

microlighting

1 Look at the photographs.
Have you tried any of these adventure sports?
Which ones would you like to try?
Which would you say are the most dangerous?
Can you think of any other adventure sports?

▲ *hang gliding*

kart racing ▼

potholing

2 Choose five adjectives which describe the sort of person who enjoys adventure sports.

impulsive   irresponsible   careful   competitive   confident
patient   mad   brave   independent

Use a dictionary for any words you do not understand. Would you use any of these adjectives to describe yourself?

1

3 **Read the questionnaire and try to guess what the words *in italics* mean in your own language.**

Have you got a spirit of adventure?

1 You would make a parachute jump:
a) Only in an emergency.
b) If it was *sponsored* for charity.
c) Only for pleasure.

2 When choosing where to go on holiday, do you:
a) Go to the same place as you went last year?
b) Choose an area popular with tourists?
c) Deliberately pick somewhere *off the beaten track*?

3 A friend challenges you to sleep in a *haunted* house. Do you:
a) Refuse?
b) Accept as long as other people stay with you?
c) Say yes without even a second thought?

4 If you were offered a good job in another country, would you go?
a) No.
b) Yes, so long as it was a short-term contract.
c) Yes.

5 When you visit a restaurant, do you:
a) Order something you've tried before?
b) Try something slightly different?
c) Order a dish you've never tasted before?

6 Would you ever go on *blind dates* with members of the opposite sex?
a) No.
b) Perhaps.
c) Yes.

7 When you have a *hunch*, do you:
a) Ignore it?
b) Agonise over whether to follow it or not?
c) Follow it up?

8 Would you ever buy a house without seeing it?
a) Under no circumstances.
b) Only if you had no choice.
c) If it was a good buy.

9 Compared with five years ago, do you:
a) Make fewer *gambles* in your life?
b) Take as many risks?
c) Take more chances?

10 Would you go to prison on a matter of principle?
a) No.
b) Perhaps.
c) Yes.

4 Match the words *in italics* with their meaning in the context of the passage:

where ghosts appear
raising money
actions or decisions which involve an element of risk
appointments or meetings with someone you do not know
somewhere not very well known
a strong feeling about something

5 Answer the questionnaire and check your score.

SCORING
Give yourself one point for each (a) answer, two for each (b), three for each (c).

10–17 points
You don't take many risks and you prefer to be absolutely certain of where you stand before deciding anything. You are cautious and have the satisfaction of knowing that your life is well under control.

18–24 points
You think about all the possible problems of every new thing you do, and make your decisions after careful consideration of the risks involved. Even so, you are not against a calculated risk occasionally as long as you won't be sacrificing too much if it goes wrong.

25–30 points
You are a true adventurer, and you believe that any project worth working on has risks which have to be taken. Progress in your life is likely to be by leaps and bounds, with the occasional backward step when a gamble doesn't pay off.

parachuting

white water rafting

6 Write two more questions to continue the questionnaire.

7 Read this passage and decide what sport it describes. Choose from the sports shown in the photographs on page 1.

When you mention the sport of .... most people imagine crawling on your hands and knees through tiny, muddy tunnels, and getting cold and wet. This is an unfair image, since .... is an exciting and challenging activity, and is certainly no more dangerous than other adventure sports.

Why do people go ....? This is difficult to explain to anyone who has never experienced the unique beauty of the underground world. Caves are fascinating places, and each has its own character — some have dark, vertical walls with powerful streams running between them, while others have large, silent chambers, beautifully decorated with stalactites and stalagmites.

How do you feel about this sport?

8 Write a few sentences to describe how you see one of the sports in the photographs. Use the passage in Exercise 7 to help you.

2 | Weather facts

1 **These pictures are all connected with the weather. In what way?**

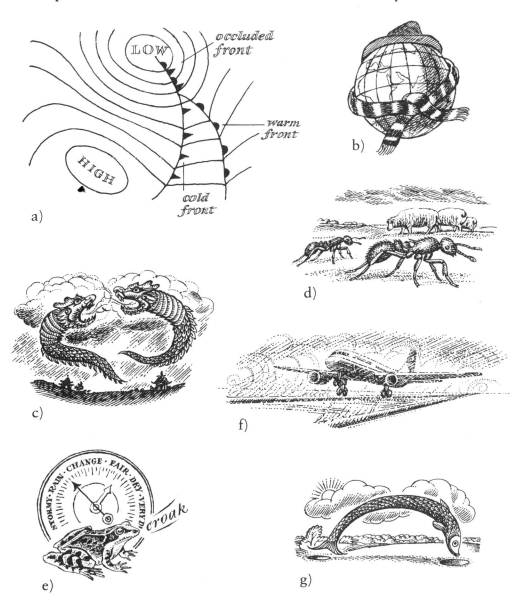

a)

b)

c)

d)

e)

f)

g)

2 Read the passages opposite. Which passages can you match with the pictures? Don't worry about the missing words for the moment.

3 Look at the word map. Check you know what each word means.

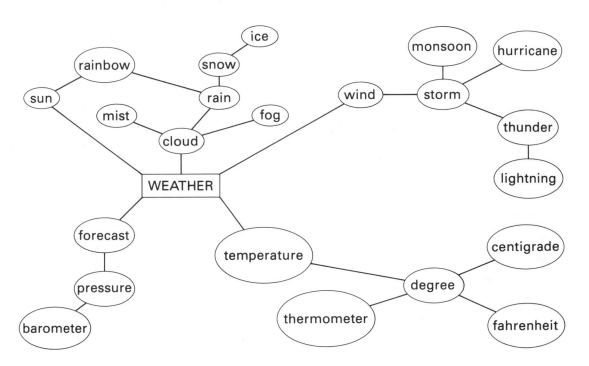

Now read the passages again. The missing words are the same in each paragraph. Try to guess what they are and use the word map to help you.

4 Answer the questions.

1 What do these have in common?
   a) the Fohn and the Sirocco
   b) frogs and ants
   c) Huitzilopochtli and Dhakhan
   d) London and Bombay
2 What prevents heat escaping from the earth?
3 How do scientists know what the weather was like in the past?
4 What causes acid rain?

5 Write down the 'weather' adjectives and verbs from the passage. Which ones go with the nouns in the word map?

1 Animals can predict the weather, often very accurately. The Germans used to keep frogs as live .... because they croak when the pressure drops.

2 One way of finding out about past climates is by drilling holes in glaciers and pulling out long cores of .... Distinct layers can be seen in the .... The darker the .... the colder the climate was. An .... core 366m long can tell us about the weather of the past 1,400 years.

3 The Chinese believed that dragons formed .... with their breath and brought rain. The rain fell when the dragons walked over the .... and storms raged when they fought with each other.

4 Most scientists think that the Earth is getting warmer. Burning coal, oil and forests increases the amount of the gas carbon dioxide in the atmosphere. This prevents the heat from escaping. If the amount of carbon dioxide in the air was doubled, the Earth's .... would rise by 2°C. If the Earth became even a few degrees warmer the ice at the Poles would melt and the sea level would rise by about 60m. Coastal cities like New York, Bombay, London and Sydney would be flooded.

5 There are two types of .... – short and long range. Computers help forecasters produce short range charts for up to a week ahead. Long range forecasting is less accurate and is often done by looking at past weather records. In India forecasts have been made of the next year's monsoon so that famine can be prevented if there is not enough rain.

6 The .... which falls on parts of Europe and North America can be more acid than lemon juice. Acid .... falls when gases and chemicals from factories dissolve in water in the air to form weak acids. Pollution carried by the wind can fall as acid .... hundreds of kilometers away and destroy forests, crops and life in lakes and rivers.

7 People were predicting the .... long before forecasts appeared on TV or in newspapers. They looked for 'signs' in the way plants and animals behave. When the pressure drops – a sign of bad .... – sheep's wool uncurls and ants move to higher ground. Pine cones open when rain is about.

8 .... can cause accidents and delays at airports. Many airports today have huge pipes along the sides of the runways. Fuel is pumped into them and burned. This raises the air temperature so that the .... evaporates and planes can take off and land safely.

9 The Aztecs believed that the .... god, Huitzilopochtli, was a warrior who fought against the power of night so that the .... could be reborn every morning. He had to be kept strong and people were sacrificed to provide him with human hearts and blood, which were thought to be his favourite food.

10 Some people say they can feel the weather in their bodies. Some people find that they have aches and pains when the air is humid. Others get headaches before a .... Some winds are said to damage your health. During the hot, dry Föhn wind the accident, crime and suicide rates in Germany rise. The Sirocco is said to cause madness.

11 The Kabi people from Australia worship a god called Dhakhan who is half fish and half snake. Dhakhan lives in deep water holes in the ground. He appears as a .... in the sky when he moves from one hole to the next.

6 Here are some sayings about the weather. Two of them say the same thing. Which are they?

Red sky at night,
Shepherd's delight;
Red sky in the morning,
Shepherd's warning.

Rain before seven,
Fine before eleven.

A *sunshiny* shower
Won't last half an hour.

If bees stay at home,
Rain will soon come;
If they fly away
Fine will be the day.

Evening red and morning grey,
Send the traveller on his way;
Evening grey and morning red,
Bring the rain upon his head.

Rain from the East,
Will last three days at least.

When the wind is in the East,
'Tis neither good for man nor beast.
When the wind is in the West,
Then the wind is at its best.

7 Do you have proverbs about the weather in your language? Do you think they are often right?

3 | A home in a foreign land

1   This unit is about the experiences of people who left their home country and came to live in England.

Look at the photograph of immigrants. Think about:

the life they had in their home country
their impressions of their new home
their feelings
the life they hope for

Can you think of other reasons why people choose to live in a foreign country?

2

Read the two passages and decide which of the following words you can use to describe each writer's experience as an immigrant:

> positive
> happy
> interesting
> sad
> humiliating
> negative

A teenage girl comes to England in the 1960s

I was born in Drummin, County Mayo, in the west of Ireland. I had five brothers, four sisters and two adopted sisters. I left school at the age of fourteen. I wanted to stay on at school as my ambition was to become a school teacher, but my parents could not afford to send me to college at that time. I went to work in a shoe factory for a year. After that I became a nanny as I wanted to work with children. I lived in with the family and worked from 8am to 8pm – for £2 a week.

At the age of seventeen I felt that there were no opportunities for me to earn a decent living and that I had to come to England. Dad gave me the boat fare and £10 to keep me going until I found a job. I came to Slough, Buckinghamshire, as that was where most of the people from my part of the country went to.

I arrived in Slough and immediately began to look around for a place to stay. I eventually found a room in Windsor. The next day I went looking for work, and found a job in a factory making Mars bars.

I had a lot to get used to in this strange country. There were big houses, trains, traffic lights and lots of people from all over the world.

I never knew the English hated us (the Irish). I did not hate them! I could not understand the hostility I received. I was not prepared for it. For example, I had to listen to people telling me how thick and stupid the Irish were. I was always told, and was made to feel, that I was different. I felt isolated and seriously thought about going back.

In fact I did go home. And stayed there for a month. But I was disappointed to find that I was a stranger there. People treated me very differently because I had been to England. I returned to Slough for a period and then moved to London in the late 1960s.

3 Read the two passages again and choose the best final sentence for each one.

   a) But I am no longer ashamed of my Irish accent and I will always consider myself to be Irish.
   b) I feel lonely here and one day I will go home to Ireland to die.
   c) As an Irish immigrant, I feel that once you leave your country, you do not belong anywhere any more.
   d) My father saw himself as an Irishman in England, but he recognised that he owed a lot to England.

An Irish girl in England in the 1960s

My parents decided to leave their small two-roomed cottage on the shore of Lough Erne, County Fermanagh, in 1960. Although my father had a steady job, his five daughters were growing up and would soon be leaving school without any employment. And so my parents took their family to England so that we could stay together for as long as possible.

I was twelve when I left a cottage without electricity, running water or sanitation for a flat in Leamington Spa, Warwickshire, which had them all. Imagine my delight at having such luxuries suddenly at my fingertips!

I went to a secondary school where I loved wearing the uniform, but I suffered terribly at the hands of mimics. My English teacher loved my unusual accent and used to make me read aloud, while the rest of the class tittered, much to my embarrassment. I joined the youth club, went swimming and used all the facilities I could afford. Where I had come from, such facilities just did not exist.

I also enjoyed going to the Irish dances, where I met lots of other Irish people. When I left school I went to secretarial college and found a good job with a central heating company where I met my husband. He is from West Cork and we travel back every year to visit his mother, who retired there after spending 45 years in London.

I am delighted that my two daughters love Ireland and keep alive the traditions by doing Irish dancing and learning Irish songs. I owe a lot to England and I get a lot of pleasure in helping out at the many different events at my daughters' school.

4 **Here are some of the words you may find difficult in the passages. They have several meanings. Decide which meaning is the correct one in this context.**

ambition: a) a desire to do something in life   b) a desire to be extremely successful
decent: a) honest   b) acceptable
isolated: a) alone   b) single
luxuries: a) unnecessary facilities   b) facilities providing comfort and pleasure

5 **Now find these words in the passages and decide what their general sense is.**

nanny: Is this person likely to be someone who teaches children or someone who looks after someone else's children?
sanitation: Electricity, running water and sanitation are basic home facilities. Is sanitation to do with baths and toilets or with furniture?
mimic: We know some people made her suffer terribly, and that it has something to do with her accent. What do you think these people might be doing?
tittered: They caused her embarrassment. How did they show this? Did they laugh? Or did they keep quiet?

6 **Write down the things that the writer of the first passage disliked and the things the writer of the second passage liked.**

7 **Have you ever felt isolated and lonely in a foreign country or a strange town? What were your experiences? What did you like/dislike?**

8 **Write a few sentences describing the impressions that foreigners have when they come to your country.**

4 | A room of my own

a)

1 Look at the rooms in the pictures. Which one looks most like a room in your house or flat?

b)

What can you say about the person who lives there?
What do you think he or she does?

c)

2

Read the two passages and match them with the pictures on page 13. There is one extra picture.

1   Fanny Waterman, celebrated piano teacher, co-founder of the Leeds International Piano Competition, draws her pupils from all over the world, and surprisingly does her best to discourage the brilliant ones from becoming concert pianists. She warns them that the life of the concert pianist can be the loneliest in the world.

The music room is the heart of the eight-bedroomed Victorian house in Leeds where she and her husband have lived since 1966. The windows lead out onto the terrace overlooking the lawn. The Steinway piano on the left, from Hamburg, was a twenty-fifth wedding anniversary present from her husband. The other had belonged to a friend. 'The Hamburg piano is the workhorse, where all the lessons go on.' She has written 22 books on piano playing; the music on the Steinway includes the latest. Next to it are Beethoven's 32 piano sonatas and nearby, Bach's preludes and fugues.

The ivory figure on the other piano was a gift to her from her father, a designer of jewellery. The vase with the flowers was a present from the young Korean Ju Hee Suh, who came second in the 1984 Leeds competition. The music stand is Victorian, while the glass dish on the table next to it belonged to the late Lord Boyle, a former Conservative Minister of Education, who became Vice-Chancellor of Leeds University. The photograph on the piano shows her with Rudolf Serkin, the pianist, taken at his summer school in 1981. There are family photographs in the window to the right . . .

3

What did the writers of the passages intend? (You may think there was more than one intention.)

a) To describe the character of the two people through their homes and their belongings.

b) To show what comfortable homes they have.

c) To give a detailed description of each person's life.

d) To show the private sides of two public people.

e) To list the contents of their favourite rooms.

2 Yehudi Menuhin moved from Highgate into his early 19th century house in London's Belgravia last July but has only lived in it for a couple of months. Born in 1917, the famous violinist and conductor, who first began his public career at the age of seven in San Francisco, still spends nine months of the year on tour. His room is four storeys up on the top floor and a lift was waiting for us in the front hall. His wife greeted us and we went to find the maestro waiting for us on the landing.

He led the way up a further flight of polished wooden stairs to his studio past a sculpture by Epstein of himself. 'This is my room and I absolutely love it.'

The idea is that the studio should look like a ship. Its walls are covered with pinewood and natural light comes in through the windows in the roof. On the floor there are cotton rugs which were made in central Asia.

The whole of one wall is covered with letters in frames, paintings and prints, mostly collected by his wife Diana. 'Anything I have of beauty or value was given to me by my wife, including herself.' He doesn't like empty surfaces. 'I need many tables.' The card table proves his point, with its neat rows of objects standing around a figure that was found in the Athens antique market.

The grand piano belonged to Menuhin's mother-in-law, who was a brilliant pianist. Rows of photographs are displayed on top. An Indian string instrument lying by the window contrasts with the record player and tape deck nearby. From the case he took his violin, a Guarnerius made in 1742 . . .

4 There may be some words which you don't understand. Choose five difficult words and follow these steps:

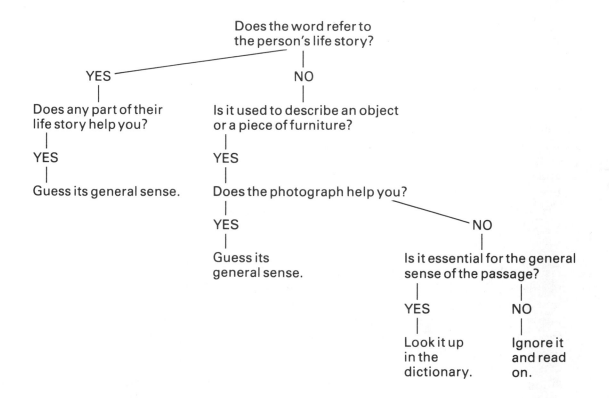

Does the word refer to
the person's life story?

YES — NO

Does any part of their life story help you?

YES

Guess its general sense.

Is it used to describe an object or a piece of furniture?

YES

Does the photograph help you?

YES — NO

Guess its general sense.

Is it essential for the general sense of the passage?

YES — NO

Look it up in the dictionary.

Ignore it and read on.

5 Find words from the passages to write under the headings below.

Parts of the house   Furniture   Items of decoration

Think of two or three more words to go under the headings.

6 Look at photograph (b) and decide what the person is like. Write a few sentences describing the room and its objects. Invent any details you like.

7 What do the objects and furniture in your favourite room say about you? Think of five items and try to remember where they came from and how long you have had them.

5 | Childhood dreams

1 When you were younger, what job did you hope to have? Have you realised your dream (or are you likely to)?

2 In the passages on page 18 some well-known people answer the question:

'When you were a child, what did you want to be when you grew up?'

◁ *Madonna*

Mikhail Gorbachev ▷

◁ *Michael Jackson*

Margaret Thatcher ▷

Woody Allen

What are or were these people's jobs? Complete the *name* and *job* columns of the chart.

Name	Job	Childhood dream
Gorbachev		

3

Read the passages and decide who is speaking.

1 'As a youngster I used to spend my holidays on my uncle's farm and for a while my thoughts turned to an agricultural career but when I went to study at the State University, I very soon got involved in the world of politics and that decided my future ambitions – incidentally it was at the State University that I met my wife Raisa.'

2 'I had an ambition as a child. I wanted to be part of the Indian Civil Service. I said: "I think Daddy, if I manage to get to university" – *if*, it was a fantastic privilege in those days – "If I manage to get to university I think I'd like to go in the Indian Civil Service because I'd like to be able to do something for them."'

3 'To dance! Sorry! But that's all I ever wanted to be. Now I desperately want to be a really good actress, but in the beginning all I ever wanted to do was dance.'

4 'I was singing and dancing at the age of five, and so were my brothers, and with my dad's guidance we spent our days in school and our nights working so I never really had the time to do anything else. My great idol was Fred Astaire. I never wanted to do anything except to perform and put everything I had into it . . .'

5 'As a child from Brooklyn, New York, the only ambition I had was to be someone else. My constant fantasy was that I'd be kidnapped. I'd get into the car with the kidnappers, they'd drive me off and send a ransom note to my parents . . . My father had bad reading habits. He'd get into bed at night with the ransom note and read half of it, get drowsy and fall asleep . . . then he lost it! Meanwhile the kidnappers take me to New Jersey, and my parents finally realise that I'm kidnapped and they snap into action – they rent out my room! The ransom note says for my father to leave one thousand dollars in a hollow tree in New Jersey. He has no trouble raising a thousand dollars, but he hurts his back carrying the hollow tree!'

4 Complete the *Childhood dream* column of the chart in Exercise 2.

5 Here are some of the words which you may find difficult. Answer the questions. There may be some other words which you don't understand. Use your dictionary to help you.

privilege: To go to university in those days was unusual. Is it likely to be a special advantage or a disadvantage?

guidance: Is his 'dad' likely to be advising or helping, or stopping him from doing what he wanted to do?

idol: Is this likely to be someone you like a lot or dislike?

snap into action: When they get the note, do his parents act slowly or quickly?

6 Which people realise their ambitions? Which person is not serious in his or her reply? Do any of these childhood dreams surprise you?

7 Read the next passage and decide what the writer's job is.

'Childhood was an illusion and the illusion was this: everything was bigger. No, I mean *everything*, not just houses and shops and grown-ups, but colours and flowers and journeys, especially journeys which seemed endless. "Are we there yet, Daddy?"

Funfairs were huge things that spread for miles around you with noise and lights and exciting danger. Rainy days at home when you were ill seemed to last for ever. Being an adult yourself was an unthinkable distant possibility. Every sound was louder, every game was grander, every pain unbearable.

As I've grown old, life has become smaller. Flavours have dulled. Surprises have turned into shocks. Days go by unsavoured. How can I recapture childhood when it was an illusion?

I have only one repeatable and precious way and even in this way I can regain only the echoes of that larger world. I can play upon the stage like a child and make the crowd laugh and laugh with them, sometimes helplessly like a child, and then, even though I'm a sixty-one-year-old, I can almost catch the colours and sounds and silliness of those bigger years when I was little.'

8 The writer says *everything was bigger*. What things seemed different to him when he was a child and in what way?

9 Choose the best summary:

1 When he was a child, the writer didn't like travelling because the journeys always seemed endless. Now he is an adult, life is less exciting but because he is a comedian he can still behave like a child when he is on stage.

2 For the writer, childhood reality was an illusion. His senses seemed sharper and everything around him seemed bigger when he was little. In comparison, adult life is disappointing, and the only time he can see it through a child's eyes again is when he is on stage making people laugh.

3 The writer didn't dream about what he would be when he grew up because being an adult was something that he couldn't imagine. He became a comedian in order to go on living in a child's world.

10 How does the writer feel about his childhood?

He is glad it is over.
He is nostalgic.
He is indifferent.

11 Think of a smell, a taste and a sound which you remember from your childhood. Can you find these sensations today?

6 | Mr Jones

1 Write a few sentences to describe one of the men in the picture.

2 Read the first part of the short story 'Mr Jones' by Truman Capote. Decide which of the men in the picture is Mr Jones.

During the winter of 1945 I lived for several months in a rooming house in Brooklyn. It was not a shabby place, but a pleasantly furnished, elderly brownstone, kept hospital-neat by its owners, two maiden sisters.

Mr Jones lived in the room next to mine. My room was the smallest in the house, his the largest, a nice big sunshiny room, which was just as well, for Mr Jones never left it: all his needs, meals, shopping, laundry, were attended to by the middle-aged land-ladies. Also, he was not without visitors; on the average, a half-dozen various persons, men and women, young, old, in-between, visited his room each day, from early morning until late in the evening. He was not a drug dealer or a fortune-teller; no, they just came to talk to him and apparently they made him small gifts of money for his conversation and advice. If not, he had no obvious means of support.

I never had a conversation with Mr Jones myself, a circumstance I've often since regretted. He was a handsome man, about forty. Slender, black-haired, and with a distinctive face; a pale, lean face, high cheekbones, and with a birthmark on his left cheek, a small scarlet defect shaped like a star. He wore gold-rimmed glasses with pitch-black lenses; he was blind, and crippled, too – according to the sisters, the use of his legs had been denied him by a childhood accident, and he could not move without crutches. He was always dressed in a crisply pressed dark grey or blue three-piece suit and a subdued tie – as though about to set off for a Wall Street office.

3

What evidence is there for the following statements?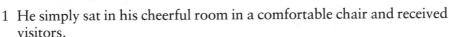

1 Two ladies looked after Mr Jones.
2 The writer didn't know Mr Jones very well.
3 Mr Jones was not lonely.
4 He couldn't walk easily.
5 He dressed smartly.
6 He earned his living by giving people advice.

4

Choose five difficult words from the passage and ask yourself these questions.

– What part of speech is the word?
– Do the sentences around the word help you?
– Are there any other words to help you?
– Can you guess the meaning of the word?

Check with your dictionary if you are still uncertain.

5

Read the next part of the story. Put these sentences in the right position:

1 He simply sat in his cheerful room in a comfortable chair and received visitors.
2 It rang constantly, often after midnight and as early as six in the morning.
3 Several months later I returned to the house to collect a box of books I had stored there.
4 But he was gone.

However, as I've said, he never left the premises. I had no idea why they came to see him, these rather ordinary-looking folk, or what they talked about, and I was far too concerned with my own affairs to much wonder over it. When I did, I imagined that his friends had found in him an intelligent, kindly man, a good listener in whom to confide and consult with over their troubles: a cross between a priest and a therapist.

Mr Jones had a telephone. He was the only tenant with a private line.

I moved to Manhattan. While the landladies offered me tea and cakes in their lace-curtained 'parlor', I inquired of Mr Jones.

The women lowered their eyes. Clearing her throat, one said: 'It's in the hands of the police.'

The other offered: 'We've reported him as a missing person.' The first added:

'Last month, twenty-six days ago, my sister carried up Mr Jones's breakfast, as usual. He wasn't there. All his belongings were there.'

'It's odd –'

'– how a man totally blind, a helpless cripple . . .'

6

How do you think the story ends? Think about these questions to help you guess.

1 Was Mr Jones really blind and crippled?
2 Did people pay him just for giving them advice?
3 Why do you think he disappeared?
4 Where did he go?

7

Now read the end of the story.

Ten years pass.

Now it is a zero-cold December afternoon, and I am in Moscow. I am riding in a subway car. There are only a few other passengers. One of them is a man sitting opposite me, a man wearing boots, a thick long coat and a Russian-style fur cap. He has bright eyes, blue as a peacock's.

After a doubtful instant, I simply stared, for even without the black glasses, there was no mistaking that lean distinctive face, those high cheekbones with the single scarlet star-shaped birthmark.

I was just about to cross the aisle and speak to him when the train pulled into a station, and Mr Jones, on a pair of fine sturdy legs, stood up and strode out of the car. Swiftly the train door closed behind him.

Were your guesses in Exercise 6 correct?

8

Look again at the man in the picture. How does he compare with what we know about Mr Jones at the end of the story? What do you think his job was?

7 | Avoiding close encounters

1   Look at the animals in the pictures. What would you do if you met one of these animals in the wild?

Imagine you are walking and camping in an area where there are wild bears.
Write down five things you should or should not do.

2 Read the advice on how to avoid bear attacks that visitors to the Denali National Park in Alaska are given. Check if you guessed correctly in Exercise 1.

Grizzly and black bears in Denali National Park can kill you or severely maul you. They are unpredictable and will defend themselves, their young, their food, and their territory. When surprised, they may react by attacking. ALL bears are potentially dangerous. Remember, when you enter the Park, YOU are the visitor.

BEAR COUNTRY: STEPS TOWARD TRAVELING SAFELY

A basic knowledge of bears, their behavior and habitat is essential if you want to travel safely in bear country.

1 Avoid coming into contact with bears.
2 Watch for the bears and signs of bears.
3 Do not feed animals.
4 Make noise.
5 Leave your dog behind.
6 Keep a clean camp.
7 Keep yourself clean.
8 Encountering a bear – NEVER RUN.

3 Match the details below with the 'Steps toward traveling safely'.

a) Talk, ring a bell, shake pebbles in a can to let the bear know where you are.
b) Stay alert and look ahead. Bear tracks are unmistakable – a five-toed footprint, as long as yours, but almost twice as wide.
c) Be ready to pack up everything and leave in 60 seconds. Cook and store food in bear-resistant containers away from your camp. Don't leave anything behind.
d) Change your route if necessary. Keep your distance at all times. Even at 100 yards a bear may begin to feel crowded.
e) You can't outrun a grizzly.
f) Pets are not part of this natural ecosystem and may attract bears.
g) Animals fed by people may lose their natural food-finding instincts and their fear of people.
h) Do not use perfumes or deodorants while hiking. Keep your clothes and equipment free of food odors.

4 **Find these words in the text in Exercise 3. Can you guess what they mean?**

pebbles: What can you find outdoors which will make a noise when you shake them in a can?

stay alert: What's the general idea of the advice? Relax and enjoy yourself or pay careful attention to everything around you?

outrun: The advice says this is something which you can't do. Does it mean run faster or more slowly?

odors: If clothes and equipment were in contact with food, how would this attract bears?

5 **Read this extract from *Three Summers: A Journal* by Yvonne Pepin. Which paragraphs describe what you can see in the pictures?**

June 26

Paralysis overcame me last night as I was reading before the fire: a strange clomp-clomp noise on the porch outside announced an unexpected visitor. When I looked up from the page, I came face to face with a bear looking in the window. It stood on its back legs, only a thin pane of glass between us. I grabbed the fire poker and ran up into the loft, pulling the ladder up behind me.

The bear must have been as frightened of me as I was of him because I heard him dash off the porch. I waited a while, went quickly back down to put out the lamp, then back up again. I kept the ladder upstairs all night and slept badly, thinking the bear would be back any minute.

July 9

The bear or bears were back last night. They didn't get what little food I had left, but they did clamber about on the porch. I discovered claw marks on the wooden board that I had fixed over the window . . .

July 12

. . . I ran into a bear cub this afternoon. On my way to the car we just crossed each other's path. I could have reached out and stroked him. In fact, this was my first reaction, he looked so friendly and cuddly. Fortunately, I knew better, one thing I learnt from a Disney film: never play with a bear cub because the mama is always nearby. She was. I saw her cross the creek and lumber up the hill as I ran to the cabin and slammed the door behind me . . .

a)

b)

6 At the end of her journal, the writer gives an explanation for the bears' familiar behaviour:

Afternote

Later that summer I was told that a number of bears had been shot with tranquilising guns in national parks where they had become a problem. The bears were transported to the wilderness behind my cabin. Accustomed to humans and human food these bears were led to my cabin first by the smell of food. Most bears in a truly wild state will avoid humans.

Look back at the advice for visitors in Exercises 2 and 3, and think about why the bears had become a problem in the national parks. Why do you think they had become accustomed to humans?

7 Are there any dangerous animals in your country? Are there any animals or insects which are a nuisance when you are in the wild? Write some advice on what to do to avoid them.

8 | School

1 The poems in this unit are about school. Think about your first day at school.

- Did the school seem far from home?
- What did the other children seem like?
- Were the first impressions positive or negative?

2 Read the poem opposite. Decide how old the person speaking is. Do you think it is a boy or a girl?

3 Answer the questions in Exercise 1 from the speaker's point of view.

4 What's the main idea of the poem? Here are some suggestions:

1 It's about a lonely child describing his or her fear of other children.
2 It's about a child describing his or her feelings on the first day at school.
3 It's about a lost child who is looking for his or her mother.

5 Read the poem again. How does the poet suggest that the child:

1 is a long way from home?
2 feels left out and alone?
3 feels trapped?
4 is very young?

First Day at School

A millionbillionwillion miles from home
Waiting for the bell to go. (To go where?)
Why are they all so big, other children?
So noisy? So much at home they
must have been born in uniform.
Lived all their lives in playgrounds.
Spent the years inventing games
that don't let me in. Games
that are rough, that swallow you up.

And the railings.
All around, the railings.
Are they to keep out wolves and monsters?
Things that carry off and eat children?
Things you don't take sweets from?
Perhaps they're to stop us getting out.
Running away from the lessins. Lessin.
What does a lessin look like?
Sounds small and slimy.
They keep them in glassrooms.
Whole rooms made out of glass. Imagine.

I wish I could remember my name.
Mummy said it would come in useful.
Like wellies*. When there's puddles.
Yellowwellies. I wish she was here.
I think my name is sewn on somewhere.
Perhaps the teacher will read it for me.
Tea-cher. The one who makes the tea.

Roger McGough

* Wellies: Wellington (rubber) boots.

6 Read 'Arithmetic' and find out:

1 who the speaker is
2 who Ron, Samantha, Carole and the baby are
3 who Mrs Russel, Miss Eames and Doreen Maloney are

Arithmetic

I'm 11. And I don't really know
my Two Times Table*. Teacher says it's
disgraceful.
But even if I had the time, I feel too tired.
Ron's 5, Samantha's 3, Carole's 18 months.
and then there's Baby. I do what's required.

Mum's working. Dad's away. And so
I dress them, give them breakfast. Mrs Russel
moves in, and I take Ron to school.
Miss Eames calls me an old-fashioned word:
Dunce.
Doreen Maloney says I'm a fool.

After tea, to the Rec†. Pram-pushing's slow
but on fine days it's a good place, full
of larky boys. When 6 shows on the clock
I put the kids to bed. I'm free for once.
At about 7 – Mum's key in the lock.

Gavin Ewart

* A list of numbers from 1 to 12 multiplied by 2, which children learn by heart at
   school.
† The Recreation ground, or park.

7 Which words best describe the speaker?

hard-working   lazy   resigned   foolish   rebellious
good-natured   difficult   unhappy   irresponsible   carefree

8 Answer these questions:

1 What is the child's role in the household?
2 How does she (or he) get on at school?
3 What kind of family is it? How do we know?

9 In each poem, do we share the child's feelings, or do we feel something else? What does the poet want us to feel?

10 Think about your first day at school and write down a few words to describe your impressions.

Do you think the words could form the basis of a poem?

11 Here is another poem about school. Read it for your enjoyment, but try not to use a dictionary too much!

Playground

The new boy standing at the school gate,
Shaking it like he was locked up inside.
He runs to the wall,
Kicks it and thumps it.
He slides down the wall,
Shuts his eyes,
Opens them again.
He stares at people as they run past,
Trying not to speak.
The bell goes and everyone runs
In except the boy.
He still stands there.
The bell goes again.
We come out –
I look at the wall.
All I see is a shadow.

Sara Barker

9 | 2010

1 What will life be like in 2010? Which of these do you think will change most? How do you think they will change?

education   transport   the countryside   clothes   architecture

What new gadgets do you think we will be using in 2010?

2 Can you guess what these gadgets are for?

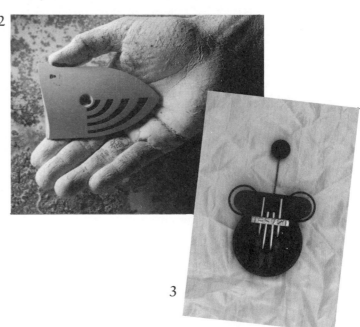

3 Read the descriptions of the gadgets. Did you guess correctly in Exercise 2?

1 The ComETel (Compact Enhanced Telecommunicator) combines a videophone with a video display screen.
2 The Sunbathing Monitor. When the sun's rays become too strong the brooch tells the sunbather to get out of the sun.
3 The Weather Forecaster uses satellites and meteorological stations to give local weather information.

Would you buy any of these devices?

4 Read the passage below and decide which of the following sentences expresses its general sense:

1 Calculators and mobile telephones are just two important gadgets that were designed in the Eighties.
2 There will be a lot more gadgets in the future because of advances in technology.
3 So many new gadgets were manufactured in the Eighties that gadget design is not likely to develop much in the future.

> There is every reason to believe that gadget design will continue to develop in the future and that the consumer of 2010 will spend more money than ever before on all sorts of strange devices. The Eighties saw very big advances in technology, which have been used to manufacture a wide range of products that you can buy in the high street, like pocket and watch computers, calculators, portable stereo units, and car and mobile telephones. By the next century, however, Eighties' gadgets will seem old-fashioned.
>
> Tomorrow's gadgets will have to be mobile, easy-to-use, compact and attractive to look at. The designs of the gadgets in the pictures have been made possible by big advances in miniaturisation techniques.

Do you have any of the gadgets mentioned in the passage?

5 Choose the best meanings for these words or expressions in the context of the passage.

consumer: a) a buyer b) business person c) shopkeeper
wide range: a) a large number of different things b) a lot of one particular thing c) something very big
compact: a) pleasant to look at b) small and practical c) colourful
miniaturisation techniques: a) electronics b) ways of making things very small c) ways of making things quickly

6 The title of the next passage is 'Cars of the Future'. Write down three questions about cars of the future.

7 Read the passage and find out if it answers the questions you asked in Exercise 6.

CARS OF THE FUTURE

What kind of car will we be driving in 2010? Rather different from the type we know today, with the next 20 years bringing greater change than the past 50. The people who will be designing the models of tomorrow believe that environmental problems may well accelerate the pace of the car's development. Today they are students on the transport design course at London's Royal College of Art.

Their vision is of a machine with three wheels instead of four, electrically powered, environmentally clean, and able to drive itself along 'intelligent' roads equipped with built-in power supplies. Future cars will pick up their fuel during long journeys from a power source built into the road, or store it in small quantities for travelling in the city.

Instead of today's seating arrangements – two in front, two or three behind, all facing forward – the 2010 car will have a versatile interior with adults and children in a family circle.

This view of the future car is based on a much more sophisticated road system, with strips built into motorways to supply power to vehicles passing along them. Cars will not need drivers, because computers will provide safe driving control and route finding. All the driver will have to do is say where to go and the computer will do the rest. It will become impossible for cars to crash into one another. The technology already exists for the car to become a true *auto*mobile.

8 Here are some difficult words in the passage. Decide what parts of speech they are. Can you guess what they mean from the context?

   pace   power   versatile   sophisticated   strips

Now match the words with their meanings in the context. Were your guesses correct?

speed
easy to change
metal lines
not simple
electricity

How many different ways are there of referring to *car(s)*?

9 Read the passage again and say what changes will make driving:

   – cleaner?
   – safer?
   – more comfortable?

10 Design your own ideal car of the future and write a short description of it.

10 | A slip of the pen

1 There are some printing mistakes in the newspaper extracts below. What should they say? Because there is not much context to help you guess difficult words you can use your dictionary if necessary.

1 ## Richard Burton to teach English at Ofoxrd

2 Sir Dallas Brooks (67) arrived back in London after nearly 114 years as Governor of Victoria, Australia. It was the longest term anyone has served in that office.

3 We find there are quite a lot of popils who come from junior schools who cannot spell properly – some of them can't even read.

4 **FIAT** for rent, own bedroom, share lounge, kitchen, bathroom.

5 ROYAL ACADEMY OF RATS
Dante Gabriel Rossetti
Painter and poet
Last two weeks

6 ## An invitation

If you feel strongly about any particular subject why not write to the 'Gazette' about it.

Or if you have a point of view to express, drop a line to the Editor. We prefer discussion on local, rather than rational topics.

7 Said 92-year-old Mr Alfred Purdle of Abbots Langley Hospital, as he looked round at the Christmas decorations from his wheelchair, "It's quite a change from the hospital. It's the first time I've been out hopping since I was taken ill over a year ago."

8 OBSTRUCTION
Michael Green, of Crimond Main Road, Danbury was fined £3 by magistrates on Wednesday for causing an obstruction with his ear in Maldon High Street.

2 The printing mistakes create some strange or absurd images. Which extract do you think is the most amusing? Can you explain why?

Choose two or three more extracts and decide if they are amusing in the same way.

3 The next extracts contain different types of mistake. Read them and find out what the mistake is. Use your dictionary if necessary.

9 Drive carefully in the New Year. Remember nine people out of every ten are caused by accident.

10 **Star's broken leg hits box office**

11 Dr Cutting said they had removed three bullets from Mr Murra – one from each leg.

12 When next you have friends to dinner one cut up in a mixed salad would be plenty for eight and a novel surprise for one's guests.

13 **BUNGALOW,** 3 bedrooms, lounge, dining room, coloured suite. Toilet 2 miles Andover.

14 1 YEAR-OLD BOXER DOG FOR SALE. Eats anything, very fond of children.

15 **Nice to feel at home**

"I spent several days in a mental hospital and felt completely at home," Christopher Mayhew MP told a meeting of the Sheffield Branch of the Mental Health Association.

16 50$ REWARD
Female Sealpoint Siamese cat. 5 years old. Very friendly, has yellow teeth. Lost on Sat 23rd. Missing from Austin Street. Could have possibly jumped into someone's car and driven off.

17 **Crash courses for pilots**

4 Look at these statements about each extract. Put a tick (✓) if it describes what the writer *intended* to say, and a cross (✗) if it describes what the writer *seems* to say.

9 Nine people out of every ten people who die by accident are killed on the roads.
10 A star actor broke a leg and threw it at the theatre box office.
11 Mr Murra has three legs.
12 Cut up one of your friends and put him or her in the salad which you can then serve to your other guests.
13 The toilet in the house advertised is two miles from Andover.
14 The boxer dog for sale eats children.
15 Christoper Mayhew thought the hospital was very comfortable.
16 The missing cat can drive cars.
17 Short intensive courses for pilots.

5 Decide what type of mistake there is in each extract.

– Missing words
– Poor sentence construction
– Confusing reference words
– Unintentional use of words with two meanings

6 Rewrite the extracts which you marked with a cross in Exercise 4 so that they describe what the writer intended them to say.

7 Do these types of written mistakes happen in your own language? What kind of mistakes can happen in spoken language?

Remember that language learners are not the only people who make language mistakes!

11 | Drawing on the right side of the brain

1   Which of these statements do you agree with?

Every normal person can learn to draw well.
Drawing is a gift that you either have or you don't have.
Learning to draw is really a question of learning to see.
The artist draws with his/her eyes, not with his/her hands.

2   The passage you are going to read is about the skill of drawing. There is a lot of difficult vocabulary, but as you read it make sure you understand the sentences which are underlined. Use your dictionary if necessary, but try not to look up words in the rest of the paragraph.
    Read the first paragraph carefully.

Most adults in the West can't draw. Other skills, such as handwriting and speech, change and develop, but drawing does not. Even intelligent and successful adults draw like children. Why?

So why do you think adults can't draw?

3   Read the second paragraph and see if you were right.

If someone was not good at reading, we would call the disability *dyslexia*. But no one has given the lack of ability to draw any special name at all, because drawing is not an essential skill for survival in our culture. Few people seem to notice that many adults draw like children, and that children give up drawing at the age of nine or ten, when they reach the stage of realism. When their drawings don't look realistic they often become discouraged. Their teachers usually tell them to look more carefully, but this doesn't help because the child doesn't know what to look for. But why doesn't a person *see* things clearly enough to draw them?

Can you answer the question?

4 Read the third paragraph and see if you were right.

Recent research shows that we use the left and right hemi-spheres of our brain for different mental functions. The left looks after speech and language, the right takes care of visual information. Sometimes the two hemispheres work together, sometimes they work separately, and sometimes they conflict, with one half trying to do what the other half knows it can do better.

So has the paragraph answered the question in Exercise 3 yet?

5 Read on and see if the next paragraph helps.

All our lives, we learn to see things in terms of words: we name things and we know facts about them. Our Western culture encourages the development of language and thinking, and therefore the left brain hemisphere. Our schools do not encourage the right brain skills of imagination, visualisation and the perception of space. It seems that the right brain takes in visual information in the way we need to see in order to draw, and the left brain takes in the same information but in a way that seems to interfere with drawing.

Write down the sentence which answers the question in Exercise 3.

6 What do you think is the solution to the problem?
   Read on and find out.

Psychologist Robert Ornstein suggests that in order to draw, the artist must 'mirror' things or see them exactly as they are. So you must turn off the left brain and turn on the right brain, so that you can see the way an artist sees. The best way to do this seems to present the brain with a task that the left brain can't or won't perform.

7 Look back at the statements in Exercise 1 and decide if the writer agrees or disagrees with them.

8 **Read the passage and try the experiments.** †

Seeing things as they really are is not so easy. Your left brain has seen and 'understood' everyday objects like the chair you're sitting on or the window and the view outside. The left brain even tries to understand and categorise strange objects as quickly as possible. But try to see things differently.

1 Stand up, turn round, bend over and look at the chair, the window and the view outside between your legs. Can you say what's different? Have the colours or the forms changed at all?

2 Look at the shapes below. Think of simple words to describe their shape.

Now look at them again and say which shape you like best. Can you say why? Can you draw it making sure it still has the qualities you liked about it? Can you draw it from the other side, so that you are in the drawing too, pen in hand?

3 Look at all these people. Can you say what they have in common?

  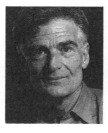 

Now can you say which person you find most attractive, and why? If you were to draw the person could you include the most subtle features which make the person so attractive?

In each experiment, you were first asked to use your left brain and verbalise what you saw. In the second part you were asked to use your right brain. Verbalising was not so easy but at least you were seeing things differently.

† Our thanks are due to Andrew Wright's *How to Improve Your Mind* (Cambridge University Press, 1987) for inspiring these activities. For more about left brain/right brain, see *Listening 2* by Adrian Doff and Carolyn Becket (Cambridge University Press, 1991), Unit 13.

9 **Which brain hemisphere do we use for these activities?**

birdwatching	inventing recipes	driving
making speeches	playing cards	enjoying good wines
collecting stamps	reading novels	doing gymnastics
making speeches	playing with children	keeping a diary

10 **Do the schools in your country favour drawing and other artistic skills? Do you think they should?**

11 **Read these quotations about drawing.**

"Learning to draw is really a matter of learning to see – to see correctly – and that means a good deal more than merely looking with the eye."

Kimon Nicolaides, *The Natural Way To Draw*

When the French artist Henri Matisse was asked whether, when eating a tomato, he looked at it in the way an artist would, Matisse replied: "No, when I eat a tomato I look at it the way everyone else would. But when I paint a tomato, then I see it differently."

Gertrude Stein, *Picasso*

"I have learned that what I have not drawn, I have never really seen, and that when I start drawing an ordinary thing, I realize how extraordinary it is."

Frederick Franck, *The Zen of Seeing*

12 | My time of life

There are but three events in a man's life: birth, life and death. He is not conscious of being born, he dies in pain, and he forgets to live.

De La Bruyère, 1688

1 **Look at the people in the photo. Decide who is most likely to be concerned with:**

earning a living
bringing up children
relationships with friends
dealing with health problems
coping with loneliness

studying
going out in the evenings
looking after the elderly
gardening
travelling

Can you think of any other matters which may concern the people in the photo?

2 Read the quotations below. How old do you think the speakers are? Are they men or women?

1 'I'm going to be the most famous actress in the world.'
2 'I do as much gardening as I can, and I also go for walks when the weather is good.'
3 'One of the most difficult things to cope with is loneliness.'
4 'When the children have gone to bed I relax in an armchair and watch the telly.'
5 'It's nice to see the kids at the weekend.'
6 'Parents can be such a nuisance! I can never do what I want!'
7 'It's a job making ends meet; kids are so demanding nowadays.'
8 'When I was young I never spoke to my parents like that!'
9 'I always have a good rest after lunch.'
10 'I never have a minute for myself.'
11 'When I get in from work I read the newspaper for half an hour.'
12 'I try and go for a run in the park at least twice a week, and when I get a chance I like to play tennis at the weekend.'

3 Read the passage opposite and answer the questions:

How old do you think the writer is?
Is the writer a man or a woman?
What does he/she do?
Does the writer seem to be happy with his/her life?

4 Some difficult words are *in italics*. Match them with their meanings in the context.

1 verb: become more numerous
2 verb: become less numerous
3 noun: imagining you are always ill
4 verb: pretend not to notice something, pretend something does not exist
5 noun: things which help make up for the unpleasant side of ageing
6 adjective: not possible to avoid
7 noun: the yellow parts of eggs
8 noun: pleasant feeling when something unpleasant is taken away
9 noun: a heavy weight or responsibility

5 What changes does the writer mention? Read the passage again and find:

– three physical changes
– one change which he/she finds disturbing
– four pleasant things about growing older

What does it feel like to be approaching the wrong end of middle age? For the moment at least, the differences between the young diplomat of 30 years ago and the ageing writer of today are more psychological than physical. Naturally, I can hardly *ignore* the *inevitable* change in my outward appearance. My hair has gone – well, silver; the whites of my eyes occasionally look more like *yolks*; and I've got heavier round the middle. But all this is merely on the surface; inside, I'm not really conscious of feeling very much older than I did in my younger days.

Mentally, however, it's another story. It is no longer a surprise to come into a room and to find that I'm the oldest person in it, but I notice the fact all the same. It's a long time since I stopped worrying about policemen being younger than me; when, on the other hand, I find generals, archbishops and High Court judges in the same happy situation, I tend to grow thoughtful . . .

Now for the *compensations*. And there are plenty of them, and by no means the least is a new found independence. Until now, responsibilities seem to have *increased* year by year; now, thankfully, they begin to *diminish*, and are replaced by new opportunities.

These are positive compensations; there are also negative ones which can be appreciated just as much. Immense pleasure can be got from Putting Things Behind One. My own recent decision – taken with immense *relief* – has been to give up all efforts to understand modern music. There is more than enough music from the 17th, 18th and 19th centuries to keep me happy for the rest of my life. Now, at last, I can face the fact that I just don't like 20th century music.

Finally, it's goodbye to *hypochondria*. When I was young I constantly worried about my health and imagined I had all sorts of terrible diseases. Now those days are over. I love every moment of my life and want it to go on for as long as possible until I become senile or a *burden* to my family and friends, at which point I would like it to stop at once. I can honestly say that I have had and am still having a wonderful time.

6 Read the next two passages and guess the missing words. You can use your own language.

One must find the source of contentment within oneself. That is one of the great advantages of old-age activities like (1) .... and (2) .... What with reading, gardening and sleeping I am far too busy to watch television. The golden rule for old age is Adapt. When you can't (3) .... to read, you can (4) .... When the weather is good, go out and garden; if you can't garden you should still go out and make the most of the sunshine. Above all, keep (5) ...., vary your interests, turn from one thing to another as the mood takes you – always have an objective ahead and Never Give In.

So, one way and another, in old age I manage to have quite a good time!

What in heaven's name have I got to look forward to? I'm very old – in my ninetieth year. I have a horrible (6) .... of old age. Everybody's dead – half, no nearly all of one's contemporaries – and those that aren't are gaga. Someone rang the other day and said, 'I want to invite you and Duff over for dinner.' I said, 'But Duff's been (7) .... for twenty-eight years.' That's what I dread.

7 Here are the missing words. Put them in the right places and check your answers to Exercise 6.

gardening   see   dead   reading   listen   dislike   active

8 Do any of the passages remind you of someone you know?

9 What are the particular pleasures and disadvantages of your age group? When do you think the happiest time of life is?

10 Do you worry about growing old? Are there things you can do now to make old age easier? Write a paragraph explaining how you would like to live in your old age.

13 | The tramp and the farmer

'The tramp and the farmer' is an old Scottish traveller's tale which was told in the evening, around a fire, after a long day on the road.

1 Look at the picture and try to guess what the first part of the story is about.

Now read the first part and check.

It was very late when the old beggarman came to the rich farmyard. He had travelled far that day, he was tired and hungry. He said to himself, 'I must find somewhere to sleep,' because it was snowing. 'I will go up here, maybe the farmer will help me. He could probably give me somewhere to lie down.' So the old beggarman walked up to the farmhouse and he knocked on the door.

47

2

Here are the key words and phrases from the next part of the story. Guess what happens.

> farmer   beggarman   cold night
> hungry and tired   barns   cattle   woods   walked
> away   closed door

Read the next part and check.

The farmer was just finishing his tea, and his wife said, 'There's someone at the door.'

And the farmer said, 'Well, I'll go and see who's there.' He walked out and there at his door stood an old beggarman with his old grey hair and his old ragged coat. And the farmer said, 'What do you want, old man?'

He said, 'Please, sir. I'm just an old beggar. It's a cold night and it's snowing. I'm hungry and tired, but just a place to lie down would be enough for me for the night.'

And the farmer said, 'You're a beggar! Old man, I need my barns for my cattle. The woods are fit for you. Go and sleep in the wood, old man, we shelter no beggars here.'

The old beggar just turned round. He said, 'I'm sorry, sir.' And he walked away. The farmer closed his door.

3

Decide if these statements are true or false.

1 The beggar is tired because he has travelled many miles.
2 The beggar asks the farmer for something to eat.
3 The farmer thinks his cattle are more important than beggars.
4 The farmer tells the old man to sleep in a shelter in the woods.
5 The farmer doesn't like beggars.

4

The sentences below come from the next part of the story. First, try to guess who the words *in italics* refer to. Then guess what happens in the next part.

1 The coachman came out of a shed.
2 '*He* told *me* to go and sleep in the woods.'
3 'It's too cold tonight. Come with *me*.'
4 '*He* will never find *you* there.'
5 'Be out early in the morning.'
6 *He* put the beggar in and closed the door.
7 *He* lay down and went to sleep on the beautiful, leather coach seat.

Now read the next part of the story and check.

But as the beggar was walking away, the farmer's coachman came out of a shed. He said, 'Where are you going, old
man?'

And the old beggar said, 'I went to ask the farmer for
somewhere to shelter for the night. And he told me to go and
sleep in the woods.'

'O-oh,' said the coachman, 'you cannot sleep in the woods,
old beggarman. It's too cold tonight. Come with me, you can
sleep in the farmer's coach, he will never find you there. Be
out early in the morning and no one will ever know you've
been there!' So he put the old beggar in and he closed the
door. And the old beggar lay down and went to sleep on the
beautiful leather coach seat. The coachman went home.

5 **Here are some phrases from the next part of the story. Put them in order and guess what happened next.**

- came to his turn
- had a dream
- went to Hell
- people that he knew in his lifetime
- Devil with a big pot of boiling lead and a ladle
- If only I had one sip of water
- boiling lead into their mouths
- burning his throat and chest

Now read on and number the phrases as you see them.

The farmer inside the house went to sleep and he had a
dream. He dreamt that he died and he went to Hell. And when
he arrived in Hell all the people that he knew in his lifetime,
who had died before him, were all sitting around waiting their
turn.

And there was the Devil with a big pot of boiling lead and a
ladle in his hand. One by one they were called up. And the
Devil poured a ladle of boiling lead into their mouths and they
swallowed it, and they were in terrible pain and crying out.
One by one till it came to his turn.

The farmer opened his mouth and the Devil put a ladleful of
boiling lead into his mouth. And he felt it going down in his
throat, it was burning him, it was burning his throat and chest.
And he said. 'O-oh God! What have I done for this? If only I
had one sip of water to cool my mouth!'

Then he looked up.

6 **Who or what did he see? What happened next? Read on and guess what the missing words are.**

And there came an old (1) .... with two cans of (2) .... He stood before the (3) .... The (4) .... said, 'Please, I beg of you! Please, give me a (5) .... to cool my mouth!'

The old (6) .... said, 'No, I cannot. Just as you could not give me one night's sleep in your barn.' And then the old (7) .... was gone.

And the farmer (8) .... in his bed. 'O-oh God, what have I done for this? That old beggar is probably in my (9) ...., he is probably smoking and setting my barns on (10) ....!' He got up from his bed.

7 **So what did the farmer do next? Read on and check.**

He walked round all the sheds on his farm. Then he saw a light in the coachhouse. He opened the door of the coach and he saw the old beggar lying there. Terrified, the farmer walked backwards out of the shed. He said, 'It's the old beggar and he's dead.'

Next morning when he got up he called for the coachman. He said, 'Coachman, did you let an old beggar in my coach last night?'

The coachman said, 'Yes, master. You can sack me if you want to. I don't care. But I could not let an old beggar lie asleep in the snow.'

8 **Can you guess how the story ends? Does the farmer sack the coachman? Is he sorry about the dead beggar? Write a few lines to finish the story.**

Now turn to page 81 of the *Answer key* to check.

9 **What do you think?**

Did the old beggarman really die?
Who was the old beggarman?
What happened to the farmer when he died?
Who is the beggar's master?
What is the moral of the story?

10 **Is there anything in the way you live or treat people which you would like to change … before it's too late?**

14 | Fear

1 **Do you get frightened easily?**
Would you be afraid in any of these situations?

- going to the dentist's to have a tooth taken out
- making a speech to a lot of people
- walking in a big city on your own at night
- being out in a violent thunderstorm
- going to sleep in the dark

Can you remember a situation when you felt very frightened? Does fear affect you physically?

2 **The passages below are about three people's 'phobias'. Read the passages and find words in your own language to fill in the gaps.**

1   The phone rang at midnight. There was a frantic voice on the other end. 'I know it's late. But it's urgent. Please come round.' My friend was standing miserably in the hallway of her flat, pointing towards a closed door. 'It's in there, please do something, but be careful, it's huge.' I opened the bathroom door carefully not knowing what to expect, and there, nestling peacefully in the plughole of her bath, was a tiny ....

2   'Going up in the lift doesn't worry me, but some of our offices have full-length windows and I feel as if the ground is coming up towards me, making me want to jump. I tried explaining my fear of .... to another girl in the office, but she laughed at me and told me not to be so silly. I know it's silly but I can't help it. I'll do anything to avoid going into those offices – I even stayed off work once when I had to go to a meeting in there.'

3   'I don't remember being at all afraid of .... at that age, but I do remember that it was a very bad .... There was lots of turbulence, even the cabin crew were falling about. I was rigid with fear for the whole journey.

   If I look up and see a .... and think about .... my heart starts beating faster and I feel sick. When I'm actually on a .... I sweat profusely and have to physically stop myself from standing up and screaming. The only way I can cope with it is to pretend it's not happening to me. I sit rigid, next to the aisle, staring at the seat in front. I can't look out of the window. I count the number of handles on the seats – anything to avoid acknowledging the fact that I'm .... It's so unnatural to be thousands of feet up with all that open space around you.'

3 Here are some words in the passages which you may find difficult. Answer the questions.

frantic: Her voice was *frantic* on the phone. Is she likely to be calm or frightened?

nestling: The spider was *nestling* peacefully in the plughole. Was it lying quietly or was it jumping about?

avoid: She'll do anything to *avoid* going in there. Does this mean she is happy to go into these offices or not?

turbulence: There was so much *turbulence* that even the crew were falling about. Would you say the weather was good or bad?

aisle: The writer sat next to the *aisle*. Did he/she sit next to the window or near the centre of the plane?

4 Read the passages again and note down the people's physical reactions to their phobias. Can you think of other phobias which cause similar physical reactions?

5 The next passage is an extract from *Nineteen Eighty-Four* by George Orwell. Read the first paragraph.

It was bigger than most of the cells he had been in. But he hardly noticed his surroundings. All he noticed was that there were two small tables straight in front of him, each covered with green baize. One was only a metre or two from him, the other was further away, near the door. He was strapped upright in a chair, so tightly that he could move nothing, not even his head. A sort of pad gripped his head from behind, forcing him to look straight in front of him.

Now think of questions to which you would like an answer.
For example: Who is *he*?

6 Now read the next part and find out if you can answer your questions.

For a moment he was alone, then the door opened and O'Brian came in.

'You asked me once,' said O'Brian, 'what was in Room 101. I told you that you knew the answer already. Everyone knows *it*. The thing that is in Room 101 is the worst thing in the world.'

The door opened again. A guard came in, carrying something made of wire, a box or basket of some kind. He set it down on the table. Because of the position in which O'Brian was standing, Winston could not see what the thing was.

'The worst thing in the world,' said O'Brian, 'varies from individual to individual. It may be burial alive, or death by fire, or by drowning, or fifty other deaths. There are cases when it is some quite trivial thing, not even fatal.'

He had moved a little to one side, so that Winston had a better view of the thing on the table. It was an oblong wire cage with a handle on top for carrying it by. . . . Although it was three or four metres away from him, he could see that the cage was divided into two compartments, and that there was some kind of creature in each. They were rats.

'In your case,' said O'Brian, 'the worst thing in the world happens to be rats.'

George Orwell, *Nineteen Eighty-Four*

7 Read the passage again and decide who or what the words *in italics* refer to.

1 Everyone knows *it*.
2 *He* set *it* down on the table.
3 *It* may be burial alive ...
4 *It* was an oblong wire cage ...
5 ... *It* was three or four metres away from *him*, *he* could see that ...
6 ... there was some kind of creature in *each*. *They* were ...

8 Answer these questions.

1 What do you think O'Brian is?
2 What does O'Brian seem to suggest by the *worst thing in the world*?
3 What was the *worst thing in the world* for Winston?

Can you guess what happened next?

9 Do you think everyone has a 'secret fear'?
What is the *worst thing in the world* for you?

15 | In search of the little people

1 **Look at the pictures of fairies. Are there fairies in your culture? Do you believe they exist?**

a)

b)

Which of these words do you associate with fairies?

pretty   dangerous   tiny   fair   cruel   ugly   dark
lovable   wild

2 **The passage opposite is about fairies. Write down what you think it may say about:**

- their appearance
- where they live
- their relations with humans
- the origin of fairies

Now read the passage and find out if you were right.

3 **Which picture above shows:**

- how people used to imagine fairies?
- how people imagine fairies now?

A cute little female about six inches high, with wings and a pretty dress is the usual description people give if you ask them what a fairy looks like. This image of the fairy as a tiny, lovable, angel-like creature dressed in white, goes back to about the seventeenth century. But before that time, fairies were very different. They were cruel and dangerous creatures which lived in the remote hills and forests of Britain.

Farmers and hunters considered them to be as real and dangerous as the wolves and bears that lived in the wilder parts of the countryside. They were feared so much that people rarely spoke out loud of 'fairies', preferring to use more respectful names such as 'the little people' or 'the hidden people'.

There were many different names for the hidden people: fairies, elves, pixies, leprechauns, brownies, and goblins, to name but a few. There were also a number of explanations of their origin. Some said they were spirits of wood and water. In Cornwall they were thought to be the restless ghosts of unbaptised babies. Still others believed them to be a separate creation, as real as humans and animals.

They had the appearance of dark-skinned and dark-haired humans, although of course they were much smaller than ordinary people. Most accounts describe them as being the size of children, about four feet or so. Their clothing seems almost always to have been green or brown, although they occasionally went naked. Many early stories indicate that they were nocturnal. They had their homes in lonely and out of the way places.

Generally the fairies hated humans and could be very cruel to them. A good example of this cruelty is the legend of the 'changeling'. The fairies would steal human babies, especially those with fair hair and blue eyes, and replace them with one of their own or just a piece of wood.

Babies were not the only thing that the fairies would steal. Tools, plates, saucepans, practically anything small that they could easily carry. Food was also taken, as well as clothing. Fruit trees were raided in the night and cows milked dry.

Sometimes relations with humans were more friendly, especially in Scotland and in Wales, where they would do household jobs and mend things around the farm in exchange for old clothes and food.

4 Find these words in the passage and choose the best meaning.

cute: a) naughty   b) attractive   c) interesting
remote: A remote place is a(n) a) busy b) dangerous c) isolated place.
accounts: a) financial records   b) stories   c) books
nocturnal: The fairies   a) lived in small groups   b) came out at night
             c) worked hard.
lonely: a) isolated   b) cold   c) high
legend: a) an old book   b) time   c) a traditional story
raided: a) The fruit trees were cut down.   b) The trees were burnt.
          c) Their fruit was taken.

5 Complete the chart.

	Modern fairies	*Traditional fairies*
Clothes		
General appearance	cute	
Size		
Sex		male or female
Character		
Home	—	

6 Read the end of the passage opposite about fairies, and choose the sentence which best expresses its general meaning.

1 The invasion of Britain by the Celts happened 2,000 years ago and folk memories prove that it has not been forgotten.
2 Fairies may not be supernatural beings at all, but they may have been the ancient inhabitants of Britain.
3 Our ancestors were frightened of fairies because they thought they had supernatural powers.

So, in other words, these were groups of small people living secretly in remote places. At night they stole food, clothing, household goods and occasionally young children from isolated farms.

The first thing we notice about these people is that their needs were not at all supernatural. They wanted food and were ready to work or steal in order to get it. Surely these were not ghosts or nature spirits.

One explanation is that stories of fairies are folk memories of the pre-Celtic inhabitants of Britain. Folk memories are oral traditions handed down over the years by word of mouth. These traditions can be very ancient.

The invasion of the Celts was an awful event for this island. It would not be surprising if some form of memory of such an important event should survive to this day. These legends survive most strongly in the Celtic parts of the British Isles: Scotland, Wales, Ireland and Cornwall.

But could stories based on these events really be handed down by word of mouth over 2,000 years?

We will never know the truth about the fairies. However, this theory does seem more probable than most.

7 **What do you think about the writer's theory of the origin of fairy stories? Could a similar theory explain the origin of any fairy stories in your culture?**

16 | Man's inhumanity to women

man /mæn/   1 A **man** is 1.1 an
adult male human being. ☐ *Larry was a handsome
man in his early fifties... He's a great President but a
remarkably boring man... Every man, woman, and
child will be taken care of... ...the first man on the
moon, Armstrong wasn't it?* **1.2** a human being of
either sex. ☐ *All men are born equal... Darwin
concluded that men were descended from apes... ...a
deserted island where no man could live.*

Collins COBUILD English Language Dictionary

1   This unit is a short introduction to sexism in the English language. First, read
the dictionary definition above. In English the word *man* has two meanings.
Do you have different words for the two meanings in your language?

2   Look at the sentences below. Does anything strike you as strange about them?

> The rich cannot possibly appreciate the effect of inflation
> on the average working man.
>
> Men have always hoped to conquer disease.
>
> Judy Chicago will have her third one-man show this
> summer.
>
> A man who lies constantly needs a good memory.
>
> Man has learned a lot. He has invented ever so many
> things. Someday he may even be able to go and visit
> other planets.
>
> A work of art is beautiful because a man created it.

Do you think that using the words *man* and *men* in these contexts affects
women? Does your language create the same effect?

3

Read the passage below. Which of the following statements are true according to the passage?

1 *Man* used to have two meanings, 'person' and 'adult male'.
2 It comes from the Latin word *homo*, meaning 'person'.
3 Today its main meaning is 'adult male'.
4 People still use it as a generic word, meaning 'person'.
5 Children and students understand *man* meaning 'person', both man or woman.
6 We must recognise that language is changing.
7 The linguistic confusion makes women seem less important than men.
8 We should stop using masculine-gender words if they also refer to women.
9 Using *man* as a generic word is misleading.

Once the word *man* meant 'person' or 'human being'. It was like the Latin word *homo*, 'a member of the human species', not *vir*, 'an adult male of the species'. But *man* has gradually become more specific in meaning and is now a synonym for 'adult male human being' only. In the words of a popular dictionary for children, 'A boy grows up to be a man. Father and Uncle George are both men.' This is the meaning that native speakers understand because they hear *man* used in everyday speech in this way from childhood.

Later we learn that *man* has another 'generic' meaning, but we do not accept it with the same certainty. Studies of college students and school children show that phrases like *economic man* and *political man*, or statements like 'Man domesticated animals' and 'Man is a dreamer' create an image of male people only, not female people or male and female people together.

To go on using in its former sense a word whose meaning has changed is unfair. The point is not that we *should* recognise a semantic change, but that in order to be precise, in order to be understood, we must. Furthermore, only recently, we have become aware that conventional English usage, including the generic use of *man* and other masculine-gender words, often hides the actions, the contributions and sometimes the very presence of women.

We can refuse to accept this view if we want, but if we do, it is like teaching children that the Earth is flat. Continuing to use English in ways that have become misleading is no different from misusing information.

4

Use the true statements in Exercise 3 to write a short summary of the passage.

5 Look at the sentences in Exercise 2. Can you write them again without using *man?*

6 Here are some more statements in which there are masculine- or feminine-gender words. Which of these refer only to men or women, and which refer to people in general?

> He who hesitates is lost.
>
> The average working man earns almost twice as much as the average working woman.
>
> Though Mary Kilpatrick is already well-known in the consumer affairs movement, she'll need the support of the man in the street now she is in office.
>
> Man can do several things which the animal cannot do . . . Eventually, his vital interests are not only life, food, access to females, etc., but also values, symbols, institutions . . .
>
> Englishmen are said to prefer tea to coffee.
>
> Margaret Thatcher won a governing majority in 1979 as Europe's first woman prime minister.
>
> Give a man a fish and he'll eat for a day. Teach him to fish and he'll eat forever.

Rewrite as many as you can, avoiding the words *man* and *men.*

7 Is there sexism in your language? Can you think of examples? Do you think you should try to avoid it if possible?

8 Enjoy these cartoons. Use a dictionary if there are any words you don't understand.

I wanted to be an astronaut . . .
but it's 'Man's Conquest of Space!'

I wanted to be a doctor . . .
but it's 'Man's Fight against Disease!'

I wanted to be the president . . .
but it's 'Man's Struggle for Power!'

Now all I want is a
self-cleaning oven.

17 | Cats

1 Cats are one of the most common domestic animals. How do people see them in your culture: as pets, as a nuisance, or in some other way?

2 The passages opposite come from a book called *A Clowder of Cats*. Read the passages and decide which ones are illustrated in the pictures.

a)

b)
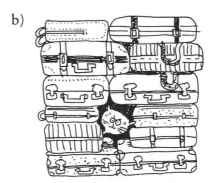

c)

d)

3 Which passage or passages are about:

a travelling cat? a useful cat?
a lucky cat? cats and the law?
a rich cat? cats and dogs?

1   A Russian legend has a story about the origins of cats. The cat's coat, it was said, was originally designed for the dog, but the dog became so impatient when coats were being handed out that he was told to wait at the back of the queue. The cat was given the fur instead of the dog. This, according to Russian folk stories, is the origin of why dogs dislike cats.

2   The record amount left to a cat was $250,000, bequeathed by Mrs Grace Patterson, of Joplin, Missouri, in 1978 to her fat tomcat Charlie Chan. He still lives in the three-bedroomed house left to him in the will, with his rent-free guardian. The antique furniture was sold to make sure he is comfortable and, when he dies, he will have a place in the pets' cemetery, which he also inherited. Charlie Chan enjoys living modestly on chicken and has no expensive gourmet tastes.

3   A nameless feline with a taste for travel flew for three weeks between New York and Tel Aviv in 1984. It escaped from its owner's cat-box in the plane's luggage compartment on the first trip and all efforts to coax it out with bowls of milk and food failed. After nearly 80,000 miles of flying the airline called in a vet who got it out.

4   The Chinese attitude to the cat was equivocal. Cats were welcome for their ability to kill mice and were considered suitable pets for women. On the other hand, they were suspected of bringing bad luck into the home.
       In the days before the invention of the watch it was said that they used their cats as clocks. The pupils of the cat's eyes were believed to gradually change shape with the position of the sun in the sky. At midday they were a narrow line and they gradually became rounder until sunset.

5   Britain's cleanest cat is undoubtedly Harvey, a five-month-old Persian who climbed into his owner's washing machine. He went through a ten-minute wash cycle before someone noticed him through the glass door, and pressed the 'stop' button. Harvey was soon back to his usual self.

6   Cats seem to be able to sense earthquakes. Josie, who lives in California, warned her family of a tremor in 1971. She woke her owners, Mr and Mrs Miller, at 5.50am by jumping onto the bed and running around. When the Millers followed her out of the house, Josie ran off. The earthquake was only a small one, but the cat raised the alarm every time there was a tremor after that.

7   In 1949 a Bill to stop cats from going out at night was vetoed by Adlai Stevenson, Governor of Illinois. The Bill required cat owners to keep their pets indoors at night. Any cat found out on the streets was to be locked up by police – if they could catch it first.
       The Governor explained that according to the law, cats were still wild animals whose nocturnal habits could not be controlled. 'It is in the nature of cats to do a certain amount of unescorted roaming,' he said. 'The State of Illinois and its governing bodies have enough to do without trying to control feline delinquency.'

8   A very fortunate high-rise cat was Gros Minou, a two-year-old ginger-and-white tom which fell 20 floors from his owner's balcony in Outrement, Quebec, in 1973. Gros Minou landed in a flower bed and suffered nothing worse than a fractured pelvis.

4

Here are some of the words which you may find difficult. Answer the questions.

bequeath: When people die, do they take their money with them or do they give it to someone?

coax: Did they want the cat to come out on its own or to force it out?

equivocal: Was the Chinese attitude to the cat positive, negative or both?

vetoed: Did Stevenson agree with the Bill becoming law, or did he try to stop it?

unescorted: Are the cats likely to be accompanied by their owners or to go out alone?

roaming: Is a wild animal one which stays asleep all the time, or travels widely in the neighbourhood?

5

Which passage do you find the most unusual? Can *you* tell an unusual or amusing story about a cat or any other animal?

6

Read the poems opposite. How do the poets feel about cats?
Choose from this list.

fear   uneasiness   indifference   dislike   affection

7

Which poem do you like best? Which one do you like least? Why?

8

Write down a few words to describe how you feel about cats or any animal you like or dislike. Can you write a short poem about them?

The Cat

Within that porch, across
the way,
     I see two naked eyes
this night;
Two eyes that neither shut
nor blink,
     Searching my face with
a green light.

But cats to me are strange,
so strange
     I cannot sleep if one is
near;
And though I'm sure I see
those eyes,
     I'm not so sure a body's
there!

W.H. Davies

Cats

Those who love cats which
do not even purr,
Or which are thin and tired
and very old,
Bend down to them in the
street and stroke their fur
And rub their ears and
smooth their breast, and
hold
Their paws, and gaze into
their eyes of gold.

Francis Scarfe

Cats

Cats sleep
Anywhere,
Any table,
Any chair,
Top of piano,
Window-ledge,
In the middle,
On the edge,
Open drawer,
Empty shoe,
Anybody's
Lap will do,
Fitted in a
Cardboard box,
In the cupboard
With your frocks –
Anywhere!
They don't care!
Cats sleep
Anywhere.

Eleanor Farjeon

18 | City scenes

1   The poem in this unit is about London and New York. Have you been to either place? Do you have an impression of them? Which five adjectives below would you choose to describe each city?

comfortable   warm   beautiful   ugly   dangerous
sophisticated   exciting   feminine   masculine   polite
elegant   civilised   fast-moving   relaxed

2   Read the poem opposite and find out if the poet agrees with you.

3   Read these lines from the poem. Find adjectives in Exercise 1 which explain the poet's impressions of the cities.

1 New York nights are like a roller coaster
2 London is a lady, fair, cool and worldly wise
3 New York is a man of steel with murder in his eyes
4 Londoners say "please"

4   Read the poem again and look carefully at the rhyme pattern. Does it stay the same throughout the whole poem? What is its effect?

What is special about each of these lines?

1 New York has a reckless risky rhythm
2 Something sweet and salty from the sea
3 Ghosts of Shakespeare, Shaw and Wilde stroll beneath the trees
4 Each has its traditions, toys and tunes

Does this have a special effect?

London Days and New York Nights

My favourite cities are London and New York
Each has its unique delights
The perfect city would be a bit of both
London days and New York nights

London afternoons are smoke and laughter
London is a brave December rose
New York nights are like a roller coaster*
New York has those bars that never close

New York is a man of steel with murder in his eyes
London is a lady, fair, cool and worldly wise
New York is amphetamine, London's charm and ease
New York grabs you by the heart, Londoners say ''please''

London has a Palace and the Tower
New York has the Lady Liberty
New York has a reckless risky rhythm
Something sweet and salty from the sea

London in the afternoon is living in a dream
Soho pubs where Behan† boozed, strawberries and cream
London treasures verbal grace, eccentricities
Ghosts of Shakespeare, Shaw and Wilde stroll beneath the
trees

London and New York are my two lovers
Each has its traditions, toys and tunes
If you want to make me happy give me
New York nights and London afternoons

Fran Landesman

* A roller coaster is a fun railway found at fairgrounds, along which people ride
  in open cars at great speed.
† Behan, like Shakespeare, Shaw and Wilde, was a man of letters.

5 **The passage on the next page is about Tokyo. Look at the opening lines of its
four paragraphs. Do you think the writer likes the city?**

Tokyo is an ugly city.
But not all is ugliness in Tokyo.
Tokyo at night is a very different place from Tokyo in daytime.
A town is not its buildings alone.

6 Read the passage and find out if you were right.

Tokyo is an ugly city. There are hardly any beautiful or even good buildings; there are very few parks; there are no mountains or even hills inside or outside the city; there is no green belt; there are few monuments worth looking at; the air pollution is terrifying; the perpetual noise deafening; the traffic murderous.

But not all is ugliness in Tokyo. There *are* a few good buildings and impressive temples and shrines; there are a few parks worth visiting. And the overcrowding, the lack of space, has one advantage, pleasing at least to the eye. Everything has to be small in Tokyo: houses, rooms, shops – even, one feels, people, to fit into the small houses. Long side-streets consist of tiny houses only, and this often creates a toy-like, unreal quality, with small women tip-toeing along in their *kimonos* and equally small men sitting, motionless, inside their tiny shops.

Tokyo at night is a very different place from Tokyo in daytime. After the offices have closed and the commuters have left town, Tokyo puts on a new face. Millions of neon signs are switched on and nowhere in the world are they more attractive, more bewitching, more maddeningly fast-moving than here. The cafés, bars and nightclubs, *sushi*-places, *yakitoriya*, Chinese restaurants and Korean barbecues, theatres, cinemas, and many other establishments open their doors. This wild, high and mondaine nightlife goes on and on and on – until 10.30 at night. Some nightclubs stay open till much later, but they are exceptions. By 11pm (earlier on Sundays) all the gaiety is over, everyone is at home and in bed.

A town is not its buildings alone; it is an atmosphere, its ambience, its feel, its pleasures, its sadness, its madness, its disappointments and above all its people. Tokyo may lack architectural beauty but it has character and excitement: it is alive. I found it a mysterious and lovable city.

George Mikes, *The Land of the Rising Yen*

7 Which of the adjectives in Exercise 1 would you use to describe Tokyo according to the passage?

8 What would your perfect city be? Does it exist or would it be a mixture of cities?

19 | Eccentrics

1 The people in the photographs can be described as eccentrics. They each have a particular interest which dominates their lives. Can you guess what these interests are?

2 Here are some difficult words used to describe the interests of the people in the photographs. Match the words with the people. You can use a dictionary if necessary.

bats battlefield battles coffin corpse fangs grave
hearse march soldier troops uniform vampire witch

3

Read this passage and guess what the missing words are. Use words from Exercise 2.

You could easily think Carole Bohanon is a (1) .... She has wild hair, ice white skin, and pale, glittering eyes that look right through you. She mostly dresses in Gothic black, and when she laughs, she reveals two long pointed (2) ....

Carole has been fascinated by vampires since she was a child: 'I know I'm not one because I'm alive, but I'd like to come back to Earth as a vampire. I believe in them, and my interest in them takes up most of my time, and all my money.'

Carole, 25, works as a graphic artist. She lives with her boyfriend in a rented flat in Surrey, and comes from a very 'normal' family. Her father was in the army, but is now a sales manager, and her mother is a home help. She is an only child.

'From the age of about four I've been obsessed with horror stories. I like the idea of a (3) .... rising from the (4) .... and have never been frightened by the supernatural. I've always been fascinated by blood. I love its colour and texture. I've never drunk anyone's blood but the idea doesn't disgust me. My parents have always thought I'm weird. Dad used to call me a (5)

................., and I'm sure in a past life I was one.'

Carole's flat reflects her interest. Her bedroom is full of (6) ...., skulls, masks and signs of death: 'If I had the money I'd sleep in a (7) .... and drive a (8) .... I saved up to have my fangs made. My canine teeth never grew properly, so I had to have my teeth fixed. I asked the dentist if I could have any shape of teeth, and when he said "yes", I asked for long pointed ones. It took months before he believed me. It's against all dental rules to make fangs.'

Carole admits that other people do not always appreciate her appearance: 'At work, I'm teased. If anyone cuts themselves, the others tell me to keep my distance. One girl had to move away from me because she was scared. I like being able to scare people. It gives me confidence and lets me get my own back for being small and a girl.'

She confesses that she has always felt different: 'At school I tried to be like the others but I felt unhappy. I'm just not interested in everyday conventions and I don't feel the need to fit in. If I didn't have to work, I'd sleep all day, and get up at night.'

Did you guess correctly in Exercise 2?

4

Choose the best meaning for these words and phrases from the passage.

obsessed: a) worried b) extremely interested c) shocked
weird: a) strange b) unhappy c) dead
teased: a) made fun of b) dangerous c) scared
everyday conventions: a) school lessons b) common phrases c) usual thoughts and behaviour.

5 Read the next passage and decide which is the most extraordinary piece of information.

Philip Coates-Wright freely admits that his obsession with Napoleon rules his life. It has cost him his marriage, eats up all his spare money, and dominates his spare time. Philip, 29, a lecturer in modern history, is a founder member of the Napoleonic Association, which re-enacts battles all over England. On field, he is a French Brigade Commander and wears authentic uniforms. The orders he gives his troops are in 18th century French. Philip even got married in a French Hussar's uniform.

His obsession started at 13: 'I had quite a cosmopolitan upbringing. My father is a heart surgeon, my mother a psychologist, and we moved around a lot, including a spell in America. My parents always encouraged my two brothers and me to have an interest and when I saw an ad in a model-making magazine to form a Napoleonic Group, I went along. There were half a dozen people and some uniforms. I put one on, marched around and it was very exciting.

Philip could not conceive of life without Napoleon: 'It dominates everything I do, and I've never had any close friends outside the Napoleonic Association. All my holidays consist in visiting European sites. I consider beach holidays a total waste of time. My ex-wife disagreed and she got fed up with my obsession eventually.'

He now lives with his girlfriend who plays the part of a male soldier on the battlefield. 'If she didn't involve herself, there wouldn't be a relationship,' he says.

Philip considers that he is eccentric: 'I don't look at things in the accepted way. Everyday life seems dull and narrow, and I think there is tremendous pressure to conform. I like to be seen as different.'

He admits there have been some difficult times: 'My parents kept hoping I would grow out of it, but I'm still growing into it! They tend to change the subject when I talk about Napoleonic Association affairs, so we're not the closest of families. It takes up 90 per cent of my life, so if they can't share it, there's not much left.'

6 Complete the chart with information from the passages.

	Carole Bohanon	*Philip Coates-Wright*
When did their obsessions start?		
What sort of families do they come from?		
How do their families react to them?		
How do other people react to them?		

7

Which of these words or phrases would you use to describe the people in the passages?

- refuses to compromise
- goes against conventional thinking
- is acting
- is fundamentally different from other people
- is an individualist
- is very selfish
- is intolerant
- is trying to attract people's attention
- is happy
- is conscious of his/her behaviour

What words or sentences in the passages helped you decide?

Can you think of other words or phrases to describe the two people?

8

Do you find the people described in the passages amusing or dangerous? Do you know anyone who is eccentric? Could you live or work with an eccentric? Do you think most of us have an eccentric habit which we hide from other people?

20 | The Misanthrope

1

You are going to read the short story 'The Misanthrope' by Slawomir Mrozek. A misanthrope is someone who dislikes or distrusts other people. Do you know anyone like this?

2

Decide which of these statements you agree with.

1 Rules and regulations are always a nuisance.
2 It is important to obey rules at all times.
3 There are circumstances when rules can be broken.
4 Rules and regulations are to help people.
5 Rules and regulations are to control irresponsible people.

3

Read the first part of the story. Decide who is the misanthrope, the writer or his fellow passenger.

The compartment was empty. I sat down by the window and opened a book. The door slid open and a man with a large suitcase came in. I returned to my reading, as I had no wish to talk. It was bad enough to lose one's privacy.

'You've got my seat.'

'Your seat?'

'Please check.'

I'd forgotten where I'd put my ticket. Eventually I found it.

'You should be occupying seat number 34 and this is my seat, number 39.'

I moved to the place opposite. I didn't want to leave the window because I like to look out at the countryside.

'Your luggage.'

'My luggage?'

He pointed to the luggage rack.

'Ah, you mean my coat.'

'That is luggage, according to the regulations, since it's occupying space intended for luggage.'

I removed my coat. He put his suitcase in its place with some effort, lecturing me meanwhile about that particular space being reserved for the exclusive use of the passenger in seat number 39.

4 Which statements in Exercise 2 do you think the writer and the fellow passenger would agree with?

Now read the second part of the story and check.

The train moved off somewhat abruptly. I was looking out of the window.

'You've taken seat number 38.'

I looked at the seat number attached to the headrest behind me and found that that was indeed the case.

'Seat number 34 is over there.'

He pointed to a seat by the door.

'Does it matter? The compartment's almost empty.'

'It's the principle that matters.'

I had a choice: I could either start an argument with this maniac or give in. He would be pleased whichever I did, though for different reasons. I therefore decided to leave the compartment.

I got up, and nearly lost my balance. The train had accelerated suddenly, and the carriage jerked. The suitcase above his head shifted almost to the edge of the rack. I realised I should await further developments.

I moved to seat number 34 without a word. It was less convenient for looking at the countryside, certainly, but it gave me a better – that is, a diagonal – view of my fellow passenger's suitcase.

The train slowed down and the suitcase retreated. I began to wonder if my calculations were correct: one had to take slowing down into account. Should I leave after all?

'As I was saying, one has to follow the rules,' he reproved me.

That decided me, and I stayed put. After all, the train hadn't reached full speed yet, and one could always hope.

I closed my eyes. Dozing is a third pleasure to be had on train journeys, after reading and looking out of the window. But I wasn't dozing. I was watching the luggage rack from under half-closed lids without attracting his attention, something I could not have done if I were either reading or looking out of the window.

5 Answer the questions.

1 What 'principle' is the man talking about?
2 Why do you think he would be 'pleased' if the writer either started an argument or left the compartment?
3 What do you think his 'calculations' are about?
4 What does he 'hope' will happen?

6 Who do you sympathise with, the writer or the other passenger?

7 Check that you understand the meaning of the following words. Use your dictionary if necessary.

curiosity   mess   swap   juggle   predestination   chaos
destiny   divine

Now read the third part of the story.

My calculations were proving correct. Slowly but surely the suitcase was moving towards the edge again. An intense understanding had sprung up between me and its centre of gravity. The moment was approaching.

And yet I decided to give him a chance. I was not moved by any humanitarian reasons, still less by the love of an individual. It was mere curiosity.

'It seems you like to obey rules. Could I ask you why?'

He grew animated. It was obviously his favourite subject.

'Rules are necessary for keeping order. Without them we'd be in a mess.'

'In that case, let me make a suggestion: let's swap tickets. Then I can take your place and you can take mine. That way we won't break the rules, as there are no names on the tickets. What do you say?'

He was taken aback, and remained silent for a while.

'But why?'

'Because I like to sit by the window. How about you?'

I was waiting. If he admitted to liking it too, he would be saved.

'But number 39 belongs to me.'

'I understand. It would mean juggling with the rules. They can't be followed to the letter, by the nature of things, but that doesn't mean one should juggle with them. Is that how you see it?'

'Well, yes . . .'

'That means you identify rules with predestination.'

'With what?'

'With predestination, with Providence. Rules eliminate a free flow of events, or chance happenings, or chaos, and are thus a manifestation of destiny, the voice of Providence.'

'I don't quite follow . . .'

'I'm saying the same as you, only using different words. You say "order", I say "predestination"; you say "mess", I say "chaos". But it comes to the same thing. To you, rules have something divine about them. Now I see why you find them sacrosanct.'

'Rules are rules, and that's the end of it.'

'Very well,' I said, and closed my eyes to indicate that there was nothing more to be said. And so it proved.

8 Which of these statements best describes how the writer feels about the other passenger at this point in the story?

1 He is amused by the situation.
2 He is irritated and just wants to enjoy the journey.
3 The situation interests him and he wants to see what will happen.
4 He is angry and he wants the man to suffer.

Which statement describes how he felt at the beginning of the story?

9 Can you guess how the story ends?

Now turn to page 84 of the *Answer key* to check.

10 Do you agree that the writer had nothing to reproach himself with? Was he right, both morally and legally?

Answer key

Unit 1 Have you got a spirit of adventure?

4 where ghosts appear: *haunted*
raising money: *sponsored*
actions or decisions which involve an element
   of risk: *gambles*
appointments or meetings with someone you
   do not know: *blind dates*
somewhere not very well known: *off the
   beaten track*
a strong feeling about something: *hunch*

7 Potholing

Unit 2 Weather facts

2 1 e, 3 c, 4 b, 5 a, 7 d, 8 f,
11 g

3 1 barometers   7 weather
2 ice   8 fog
3 clouds   9 sun
4 temperature   10 storm
5 forecast   11 rainbow
6 rain

4 1 a) They are both winds.
b) They both forecast a drop in pressure.
c) They were both weather gods.
d) They would both be flooded if the sea
   level rose.
2 The increased amount of carbon dioxide
   from burning coal, oil and forests.
3 By looking at ice cores which tell them
   about the weather in the past.
4 Polluting gases and chemicals dissolve in
   water in the air which is carried by the
   wind to fall as rain.

5 **Suggested answers:**

drops: pressure
raged: storms
rise: temperature
short range, long range: forecast
falls, acid: rain
bad: weather
hot, dry: wind

6 'Red sky at night' and 'Evening red and
morning grey'

Unit 3 A home in a foreign land

2 The writer of the first passage suggests her
experiences were rather negative and
sometimes humiliating.
The writer of the second passage describes her
experiences as positive, happy and
interesting.

3 1 c, 2 a

4 *ambition*: a)
decent: b)
isolated: a)
luxuries: b)

5 *nanny*: Someone who looks after
   someone else's children
sanitation: Baths and toilets
mimic: They might be copying her accent
tittered: They laughed

6 **Possible answers:**

1 Hostility towards the Irish, feeling isolated
2 The luxuries in her flat, the school
   uniform, youth clubs, swimming, Irish
   dances, helping out at events at her
   daughters' school

Unit 4   A room of my own

2 1 c, 2 a

3 Suggested answers

a, d, e

5 *Parts of the house*
music room   windows   terrace
lawn   room   storey   floor
lift   landing   stairs   studio
wall   roof
Further suggestions:
kitchen   bedroom
dining room   garden

Furniture
piano   music stand   tables
Further suggestions:
chair   desk   sofa
bed   cupboard   wardrobe

Items of decoration
ivory figure   vase   flowers
glass dish   photograph
sculpture   cotton rugs
letters in frames   paintings   prints
Indian string instrument
Further suggestions:
plants   porcelain
ornamental clocks   tapestries

Unit 5   Childhood dreams

2

Name	Job	Childhood dream
Gorbachev	President of USSR	a career in agriculture
Thatcher	politician	civil servant in India
Madonna	singer and dancer	dancer
Jackson	singer and dancer	singer and dancer
Allen	actor and film director	to be someone else

3 1 Mikhail Gorbachev
2 Margaret Thatcher
3 Madonna
4 Michael Jackson
5 Woody Allen

4 See the completed chart in Exercise 2.

5 *privilege*: a special advantage
guidance: advising and helping
idol: someone you like a lot
snap into action: quickly

6 Madonna and Michael Jackson have realised their childhood ambitions. Woody Allen is not serious in his reply.

7 The writer is Bob Monkhouse, a comedian.

8 Suggested answers:

Houses, shops and grown-ups were bigger.
Colours and flowers were brighter.
Journeys were longer.
Funfairs were bigger, noisier and more dangerous.
Rainy days at home when you were ill were longer.
Every sound was louder, every game was grander, every pain (more) unbearable.
Flavours tasted stronger.
Surprises have become unpleasant.
Every day used to be savoured and enjoyed.

9 2

10 He feels nostalgic about his childhood.

Unit 6   Mr Jones

2 Mr Jones is the man in the middle of the picture.

3 1 Mr Jones's *meals, shopping, laundry, were attended to by the middle-aged landladies.*
2 The writer *never had a conversation with Mr Jones.*
3 *Half-a-dozen various persons* visited Mr Jones every day.
4 He was *crippled* and *could not move without crutches.*
5 He wore a *crisply pressed dark grey or blue three-piece suit and a subdued tie.*
6 His visitors apparently *made him small gifts of money for his conversation and advice.*

5 Sentence 1 goes after ... *he never left the premises.*
Sentence 2 goes after ... *the only tenant with a private line.*
Sentence 3 goes after ... *I moved to Manhattan.*
Sentence 4 goes after ... *All his belongings were there.*

Unit 7   Avoiding close encounters

3 1 d, 2 b, 3 g, 4 a, 5 f, 6 c, 7 h, 8 e

4 *pebbles*: Stones
stay alert: Pay careful attention to everything around you
outrun: Faster
odors: By the smell of the food

5 a) July 12
b) June 26

6 **Possible answer:**

They had become a problem because they were dangerous to humans. They had become accustomed to humans because there were so many visitors in the national parks.

Unit 8   School

3 The school seemed *a million(...) miles from home.*
The other children seemed *big, noisy* and very *much at home.*
The child's first impressions were negative.

4 2

5 1 The poet uses an invented *millionbillionwillion miles from home*, which has the effect of exaggeration.
2 The other children, who are *so big, (...) so noisy* have spent years inventing games *that don't let me in.*
3 The child wonders if the *railings* are there to *stop us getting out.*
4 The child wishes he or she could *remember my name.*

6 1 The speaker is probably the eldest girl in a large family.
2 Ron, Samantha, Carole and the baby are her brothers and sisters.
3 Mrs Russel is probably a neighbour who looks after the children during the day while the mother is at work. Miss Eames is probably her teacher, and Doreen Maloney is probably at the same school as the girl.

7 **Suggested answers:**

hard-working, resigned

8 1 The child's role is to look after her younger brothers and sisters while her mother is at work.
2 She doesn't get on very well at school.
3 It's a large family, probably rather poor. The mother is working a great deal, while her father is described simply as being 'away'; possibly he has left the family or is in prison.

9 Suggested answer:

In the first poem, we share the child's feelings; the poet wants to remind us of our own first day at school.
In the second poem, the poet wants us to feel pity for the child, rather than share her feelings, which are not very obvious.

Unit 9   2010

4 2

5 *consumer*: a)
wide range: a)
compact: b)
miniaturisation techniques: b)

8 *pace*: (noun) speed
power: (noun) electricity or gas, for example
versatile: (adjective) easy to change
sophisticated: (adjective) not simple
strips: (noun) metal lines

There are five ways of referring to *car(s)*: type, *models, machine, vehicles, automobile.*

9 *cleaner driving*: electrically powered
safe driving: controlled by computer
more comfortable: a versatile interior with the adults and children in a family circle

Unit 10   A slip of the pen

1 1 OXFORD   5 ARTS
2 14 years   6 national
3 pupils   7 shopping
4 FLAT   8 car

4 9 ✓ 10 ✗ 11 ✗ 12 ✗ 13 ✗ 14 ✗
15 ✓ 16 ✗ 17 ✓

5 9 Missing words
10 Unintentional use of words with two meanings
11 Poor sentence construction
12 Confusing reference words
13 Poor sentence construction
14 Unintentional use of words with two meanings
15 Unintentional use of words with two meanings
16 Missing words
17 Unintentional use of words with two meanings

6 Possible answers:

10 The star's broken leg affected the box office.
11 Dr Cutting said they had removed three bullets from Mr Murra – one bullet from each leg and the third from elsewhere.
12 When next you have friends to dinner, a(n) (*exotic type of salad vegetable*) cut up in a mixed salad would be plenty for eight people…
13 BUNGALOW 2 miles from Andover, 3 bedrooms, lounge, dining room, coloured suite, toilet.
14 1 YEAR-OLD BOXER DOG FOR SALE. Eats anything, very good with children.
16 Could have possibly jumped into someone's car which had then been driven off.

Unit 11   Drawing on the right side of the brain

5 It seems that the right brain takes in visual information in the way we need to see in order to draw, and the left brain takes in the same information but in a way that seems to interfere with drawing.

7 Every normal person can learn to draw well. (The writer agrees.)
Drawing is a gift that you either have or you don't have. (The writer disagrees.)
Learning to draw is really a question of learning to see. (The writer agrees.)
The artist draws with his/her eyes, not with his/her hands. (The writer agrees.)

Unit 12 My time of life

4
1	increased	6	inevitable
2	diminish	7	yolks
3	hypochondria	8	relief
4	ignore	9	burden
5	compensations		

5 Three physical changes: hair has gone silver; the whites of eyes look like yolks; has got heavier round the middle

One disturbing change: notices when he/she is the oldest person in the room

Four pleasant things about growing old: fewer responsibilities, new opportunities, putting things behind one (in this case, giving up trying to understand 20th century music), goodbye to hypochondria

7
1	reading	5	active
2	gardening	6	dislike
3	see	7	dead
4	listen		

Unit 13 The tramp and the farmer

3
1	True	4	False
2	False	5	True
3	True		

4
2 the farmer, the beggar
3 the coachman
4 the farmer, the beggar
6 the coachman
7 the beggar

5
f) came to his turn
a) had a dream
b) went to Hell
c) people that he knew in his lifetime
d) Devil with a big pot of boiling lead and a ladle
h) If only I had one sip of water
e) boiling lead into their mouths
g) burning his throat and chest

6 Possible answers:

1	beggar	6	beggar
2	water	7	beggar
3	farmer	8	awoke
4	farmer	9	barns
5	sip/drink	10	fire

8   And the farmer said to him, '*Sack you?* My man, I'm not going to sack you. You can work for me for the rest of your life! Tomorrow morning I want you to get a beautiful sign made telling the world "Tramps and Beggars will be Welcome". Put it at my road end.'

So the coachman did as he was told. But the farmer waited, and he waited and he waited for many many years. Never a tramp or beggar came to his doorway until the day he died. And what happened to that farmer, I'm sure you know as well as I do.

Unit 14 Fear

2 Possible answers:

1 spider
2 heights
3 flying, flight, plane, flying, plane, flying

3 *frantic*: frightened
nestling: lying quietly
avoid: not happy
turbulence: bad
aisle: near the centre of the plane

4
1 frantic voice
2 feels as if the ground is coming up towards her, makes her want to jump
3 rigid with fear, heart starts beating faster, feels sick, sweats profusely, wants to stand up and scream

5 Possible questions:

Who is he? Why is he in a cell? Why are the tables covered in green baize? Why was he strapped in a chair? Why was he forced to look straight in front of him?

7
1 the answer to the question 'What is in Room 101?'
2 the guard, the box or basket
3 the worst thing in the world
4 the thing on the table
5 the wire cage, Winston
6 compartment, the creatures

8 1 The person who has put Winston in prison.
  2 The most frightening thing that can ever happen to someone.
  3 Rats, which he was frightened of.

Unit 15   In search of the little people

3 how people used to imagine fairies – Picture b)
how people imagine fairies now – Picture a)

4 *cute*: b)   *lonely*: a)
remote: c)   *legend*: c)
accounts: b)   *raided*: c)
nocturnal: b)

5

	Modern fairies	*Traditional fairies*
Clothes	pretty white dress	dressed in green or brown, occasionally naked
General appearance	cute, wings, angel-like	dark-skinned, dark-haired
Size	six inches high	about four feet tall
Sex	female	male or female
Character	lovable	cruel, dangerous
Home	–	remote hills and forests of Britain

6 2

Unit 16   Man's inhumanity to women

3 True: 3, 4, 6, 7, 8, 9

5 Possible answers:

The rich cannot possibly appreciate the effect of inflation on the average working person / worker.
Human beings / Women and men have always hoped to conquer disease. OR The conquest of disease has always been a goal of human societies.
Judy Chicago will have her third one-woman / solo show this summer.

Someone who lies constantly needs a good memory.
As human beings, we have learned a lot. We have invented ever so many things. Someday we may even be able to go and visit other planets.
A work of art is beautiful because a human being created it.

6 The sentences which refer to people in general can be rewritten:

People who hesitate are lost.
Though Mary Kilpatrick is already well-known in the consumer affairs movement,

she'll need the support of the ordinary
person / voter now she is in office.
Human beings can do several things which
animals cannot do… Eventually their vital
interests are not only life, food,
relationships with others / access to
members of the opposite sex, etc., but also …
The English are said to prefer tea to coffee.
Give someone a fish and they'll eat for a day.
Teach them to fish and they'll eat forever.

Unit 17   Cats

2 1d, 3b, 5a, 6c

3 a travelling cat: 3
a lucky cat: 5, 8
a rich cat: 2
a useful cat: 4, 6
cats and the law: 7
cats and dogs: 1

4 *bequeath*: Give to someone
coax: To come out on its own
equivocal: Both
vetoed: He tried to stop it
unescorted: To go out alone
roaming: Travels widely

6 **Suggested answers:**

The Cat: uneasiness
Cats (Farjeon): dislike
Cats (Scarfe): affection

Unit 18   City scenes

3 **Suggested answers:**

1 exciting, fast-moving
2 beautiful, sophisticated, feminine, elegant,
civilised, relaxed
3 ugly, dangerous
4 polite, civilised

4 The rhyme pattern changes in stanzas 3 and
5, which perhaps reflects the difference
between the two cities.
   Each line repeats certain sounds, which
emphasises the rich variety of adjectives that
can be used to describe the two cities.

Unit 19   Eccentrics

3 1 vampire   5 witch
2 fangs   6 bats
3 corpse   7 coffin
4 grave   8 hearse

4 *obsessed*: b)
weird: a)
teased: a)
everyday conventions: c)

6

	Carole Bohanon	Philip Coates-Wright
When did their obsessions start?	When she was a child	At the age of 13
What sort of families do they come from?	Very 'normal'	Cosmopolitan
How do their families react to them?	They think she's 'weird'	They change the subject when he talks about the NA
How do other people react to them?	They don't always appreciate her appearance, and tease her or are frightened	His ex-wife got fed up with him, his girlfriend involves herself

Unit 20   The Misanthrope

3 The misanthrope is probably the fellow passenger.

4 The writer: 3, possibly 1
The fellow passenger: 2, 4, 5

5 1 The principle of sitting in the right seat.
2 If the writer started an argument, the other passenger would not be defeated; if the writer left the compartment, the other passenger would also win.
3 He has calculated that the movement of the train might move the suitcase closer to the edge of the rack.
4 That the suitcase might fall on the man's head.

8 3 at this point in the story
2 at the beginning

9   When the suitcase fell, the metal corner hit him on the head, and he slid to the floor. I thought he'd been knocked unconscious and I swear I didn't want that to happen, if only because I didn't know what to do. How does one revive an unconscious person? What a bother! I looked round helplessly and saw the handle with its notice 'Pull in case of emergency'. It was indeed an emergency; and he needed first aid fast. I pulled.

The train was delayed for two hours as a result, which caused chaos in the timetables of the entire area. The disruption served no purpose in the end, since it transpired that he had been killed outright.

I had nothing to reproach myself with: I had followed the rules throughout.

To the teacher

The primary aim of *Reading 2* is to help the learner develop the skill of reading English. The means of achieving this aim are many, but probably the most important is *learner motivation*. Reading in the mother tongue is such an enjoyable activity that it would seem highly desirable to recreate this enjoyment when the student starts to read in the foreign language. But the motivation to read in the mother tongue may often be different from the motivation to read in the foreign tongue.

The reader in the mother tongue has a reason for reading and the consequent motivation is self-directed. The reason may sometimes be spurious or ephemeral, but at least this reader is in control and can choose what he or she wants to read. But in the foreign language, reading is often a classroom activity, and may be directed and controlled by the teacher. This reader is often told either implicitly or explicitly what to read and how. So how does the teacher in the artificial situation of the classroom recreate the motivation for, and enjoyment of reading that the reader would normally experience in real life?

There seem to be three key factors in stimulating the learner's motivation: the text, the task and the teacher's role. In *Reading 2* we have tried to incorporate these three factors in an attempt to make reading enjoyable and motivating.

The text

The type of texts we choose for use in the classroom has an obvious and important role to play in stimulating learner motivation. We have tried to choose material which was varied, interesting and intellectually stimulating to as many people as possible. It does not seem a satisfactory way of promoting motivation to use material which contains familiar ideas and information and in which the only interest is in deciphering the foreign language.

Many of the texts contain some vocabulary which will be unfamiliar to the learner. When we were selecting the texts, it seemed important to us to use as much authentic material as possible, that is to say, material which was not especially written for language learners. We feel that the learner should be exposed to real-life, roughly graded English at as early a stage as possible. We have avoided all carefully graded texts which would pose little or no comprehension difficulties and which would not necessarily develop the learner's reading skills.

Motivation through the text and its content was a primary objective. But realistically, it seems unlikely that a text will interest all of the people all of the time. Another factor seems essential in stimulating motivation: the task.

The task

The tasks or activities which accompany the texts in *Reading 2* have two intentions: the first is to create or maintain learner motivation; the second is to develop the useful microskills for reading.

We have already said that a text and its content will rarely be able to bear the full responsibility for stimulating genuine learner motivation. But if it is accompanied by interesting tasks, we feel that learner motivation can be created and maintained artificially. The classroom context remains artificial and few of the tasks in *Reading 2* could be said to be real-life tasks; we do not usually have to match headings, pictures and paragraphs, or unscramble sentences when we read a novel or a magazine! Yet these kinds of tasks may be problem-solving activities or stimuli for discussion; they are not always linguistically complex, but are often conceptually difficult, and therefore enjoyable and motivating in their own right.

The microskills for reading which are presented in *Reading 2* are developed using a variety of different activity types.

Extracting main ideas   It is important to help the learner look for the main ideas of a passage and to avoid getting distracted by unfamiliar vocabulary. Typical activity types which develop this skill are matching exercises; text with picture, text with heading, etc. Sometimes, there may be an extra sentence, or an extra picture. This only makes the reader think a bit more!

Understanding text organisation   It is sometimes difficult to understand what information is important in a passage and where it should come. Text organisation activities help the reader to see what belongs to a passage, and how sentences are joined together in a logical way.

Inferring   A writer may want you to understand more than the actual words you read. Inferring activities draw the reader's attention to the overall atmosphere of the passage. They also help build their vocabulary.

Predicting   Before learners read a text, it may be helpful to encourage them to look at the subject or the title of the passage, and to think about the possible content. But remember: it doesn't matter if the learners do not predict correctly. The activity still helps prepare them for reading.

Dealing with unfamiliar words   In this book there will be many words which the learner will not understand. This is because all the passages are examples of real-life written English. It is important to try and guess the general sense of a difficult word, and there are a number of activities which help the reader deal with unfamiliar vocabulary without using dictionaries or asking the teacher to explain or translate.

Reading for specific information   We sometimes read to find the answer to a particular question, and not to understand the general sense of the passage.

There are a number of exercises like this to help the learner read for specific information.

Linking ideas   Often a writer uses several different words to describe the same idea. Sometimes the use of a pronoun, for example, may be confusing, although the context usually makes the meaning clear. This type of exercise concentrates on the words used to link ideas.

Evaluating the text   In order to understand a text more thoroughly, the reader may need to appreciate the writer's viewpoint and the reason it was written, as well as to distinguish between facts and opinions. The exercises which develop this particular microskill help to develop the learner's more critical faculties.

Reacting to the text   In order to engage the readers' interest in a text, it is useful to encourage them to react in a more subjective way to, for example, its humour or its literary and poetic appeal. The readers' reactions to other text types, such as instructions, may be registered by them carrying out the instructions and demonstrating their comprehension in a non-verbal way. This skill may also develop their ability to supply missing context and information about the text.

However, it has to be said that one disadvantage of giving too much importance to microskills is that the learner may already have acquired some or all of them. In this case, they should be seen as devices for motivating the learner.

The teacher's role

Motivation is a most elusive factor in learning: we know it facilitates learning, but we don't quite know how to stimulate it, even though we all know for sure when we are addressing motivated learners. Our attempt in *Reading 2* has been to use as many different texts and tasks as possible to achieve this. But ultimately, the teacher has the final responsibility in making sure the learner remains happy and interested in his or her work by being flexible about the teaching material to be used. As a teacher using *Reading 2*, you can:

- either work through each unit in order or choose only those which are likely to interest your students. You may not have time to do every unit, and not every unit will interest everyone.
- either do every exercise, or only do those which are useful or interesting to the students.
- either start at the beginning of the book and work through to the end, or choose to do units in random order. There is no particular grading in the book, although the texts at the beginning tend to be linguistically less complex than those at the end.
- let the students work alone, or in pairs.
- let the students choose the texts which interest them, or direct them to particular units.
- choose units which cover language points or themes that are related to the main syllabus of your course.

- extend the work covered in the unit with further discussion or writing practice.
- help learners to read actively if you avoid translating or explaining every single item of vocabulary which they do not understand.

Finally, remember that this book is designed to help you teach, and to help your learners learn. It is a framework for reading practice, and not a straitjacket. Don't hesitate to adapt the material if you so choose. We hope you and your students enjoy using *Reading 2*.

Acknowledgements

The authors and publishers are grateful to the following for permission to reproduce copyright material. It has not been possible to identify the sources of all the material used and in such cases the publishers would welcome information from copyright owners.

Robert Harding Picture Library and A.C. Waltham for the potholing photograph on p. 1; Colorsport for all the other photographs on pp. 1 and 3; *best* magazine for the questionnaire on p. 2; Usborne Publishing for the extract on p. 7 from *The Usborne Book of Facts and Lists*; Topham Picture Library for the photographs on pp. 9 and 13; Trentham Books Ltd for the extracts on pp. 10 and 11 from *The Irish* by Tom Arkell; *The Observer* for the extracts on pp. 14, 15, 33 and 34; Associated Press/Topham Picture Library for the photographs of Madonna, Gorbachev, Michael Jackson and Woody Allen on p. 17; Link Picture Library and Gavin Crilly for the photograph of Margaret Thatcher on p. 17; Ring Press Books for the extracts on pp. 18 and 19 from *Child Lines*, edited by Peter Langridge; Random House, Inc. for the extracts on pp. 21, 22 and 23 from *Music for Chameleons* by Truman Capote, copyright © 1975, 1979, 1980 by Truman Capote; Frank Lane Picture Agency for the photographs on p. 24; Denali National Park and Preserve, Alaska for the extracts on p. 25; Yvonne Pepin and Shameless Hussy Press for the extracts on pp. 26 and 27 from *Three Summers: A Journal* by Yvonne Pepin; Penguin Books for 'First Day at School' by Roger McGough on p. 29 and 'Arithmetic' by Gavin Ewart on p. 30 from *Strictly Private – An anthology of poetry chosen by Roger McGough*; Pirate Design for the photographs on p. 32; *Private Eye* for the extracts on pp. 36 and 37 from *Private Eye's Bumper Book of Boobs*; the extracts on pp. 39 and 40 © 1989 by Betty Edwards, from the book *Drawing on the Right Side of the Brain* and reprinted with special permission from Jeremy P. Tarcher, Inc., Los Angeles and Souvenir Press Ltd; Jeremy Pembrey for the three left-hand photographs on p. 41; Link Picture Library and Ingrid Gavshon for the photograph (right) on p. 41; Sally and Richard Greenhill for the photograph on p. 43; Times Newspapers Ltd for the extracts on pp. 45 and 46 from articles by Lord Norwich and A.L. Rowse in 'My Time of Life' (*Sunday Times Magazine*, 26 April 1987) © Times Newspapers Ltd 1987, and from an interview with Lady Diana Cooper by Michael Roberts, (*Sunday Times*, 20 September 1981) © Times Newspapers Ltd 1981; Canongate for the extracts on pp. 47, 48, 49, 50 and 81 from *May the Devil Walk Behind Ye! Scottish Traveller Tales* by Duncan Williamson; *Woman's World* for the extract on p. 51; A.M. Heath & Co. Ltd, the estate of the late Sonia Brownell Orwell and Martin Secker & Warburg Ltd and Harcourt Brace Jovanovich, Inc. for the extracts on pp. 52 and 53 from *Nineteen Eighty-Four* by George Orwell, © 1949 by Harcourt Brace

Jovanovich, Inc., renewed 1977 by Sonia Brownell Orwell; Simon Webb for the extracts on pp. 55 and 57 from *Prediction* magazine; Collins Publishers for the definition on p. 58 from the *Collins COBUILD English Language Dictionary*; The Women's Press for the extracts on pp. 58, 59 and 60 from *The Handbook of Non-Sexist Writing* by Casey Miller and Kate Swift; Abner Stein for the cartoon by Rhea Banker on p. 61, © 1977; Futura for the extract on p. 63 from *A Clowder of Cats* by Graham and Sylvana Nowin; the Board of Trustees of the Victoria and Albert Museum for the illustration on p. 64; Mrs H.M. Davies and Jonathan Cape Ltd for 'The Cat' by W.H. Davies on p. 65, from *The Complete Poems of W.H. Davies*; Oxford University Press for 'Cats' by Eleanor Farjeon on p. 65, from *The Children's Bells*; Francis Scarfe for 'Cats' on p. 65, from *Forty Poems and Ballads*; Jay Landesman Ltd for 'London Days and New York Nights' by Fran Landesman on p. 67; A.M. Heath & Co Ltd for the extract on p. 68 from *The Land of the Rising Yen* by George Mikes; *Living* magazine for the extracts and photographs on pp. 69, 70 and 71 from 'What an eccentric lot we are' by Michelle Jaffe Pearce and Judy Goldhill; Brombergs Bokförlag AB for the text on pp. 73, 74, 75 and 84 of 'The Misanthrope' by Slawomir Mrozek, © Slawomir Mrozek.

Drawings by Julie Anderson, Peter Brown, Lisa Hall, Helen Herbert, Leslie Marshall, Chris Rothero and Shaun Williams.
Artwork by Peter Ducker and Hardlines.
Book designed by Peter Ducker MSTD.